CW01334178

July 1999
To Win and George
Alfred Gehn Pengelly

OH, FOR A FISHERMAN'S LIFE

An Autobiography

by

Alfred John Pengelly B.E.M.

I dedicate this book to my wife Eileen who, through the years of depression in the fishing industry during our married life, had the very much harder task of keeping the home and family together, fed and clothed, and could probably write better than I of the real hardships of those days.

To all my friends and shipmates, whose names may not have been mentioned but are nevertheless a part of this story, God bless you all and thanks for the memories.

* * * * * * * * * * *

My sincere thanks to all who have helped me to compile this book.

To my daughter Julie for the typewritten sheets she produced from my badly handwritten manuscript.

For report on shark fishing by John Stevens of the Marine Biological Association, Plymouth.

For statistics on landings by Brian Tudor, Secretary of the Shark Angling Club of Great Britain.

For mackerel landings by David Pengelly, Manager, Cornwall Fishermen Limited, Looe Branch.

For photographs by kind permission of:
- *Beken & Son, Cowes*
- *Morris Rosenfeld*
- *Austin Toms*
- *Arthur Collings*
- *Albert Stephens*
- *Fisher Barham*
- *A.E. Raddy & Son, Looe*
- *Charles Schribners, London*
- *Clarence Seccombe*
- *Mrs. June Webb (nee Middleton)*
- *Jack Edwards*
- *Royal Institute of Cornwall.*

Finally my very grateful thanks to Kevin Crucks, British Broadcasting Corporation for his advice.

© **Alfred John Pengelly 1979**

Designed by Fisher Barham, Falmouth

Printed by Century Litho, Falmouth

Bound by Booth Binders, Mabe, Falmouth

PUBLISHED BY
GLASNEY PRESS, FALMOUTH

CONTENTS

Introduction	6. 8.
Childhood Memories and Escapades	13. 15. 19. 21.
Mackerel's Up!	24. 25.
I Start my Seafaring Career — Ashore!	28. 29. 31.
Caught in the Wolf Rock	34. 37. 38.
Yachting	40. 42. 45. 46.
Shamrock V	48. 51. 52. 54.
The America's Cup	56. 58. 60.
The Choir, then Back to Shamrock	62. 64. 66.
New Responsibilities, then War	67. 69. 70. 71.
Helping to fill the Nation's Larder	72. 73.
Post War Troubles and Trials	75. 76. 78.
The Shark Fishing and Pleasure Trade Expands	85. 86. 88. 89.
Marketing the Catch	91. 92.
In Conclusion	95. 96. 98. 99.
Looe Built Luggers	101.
Looe Fishermen's Nicknames	103.

Above: General view of East Looe circa. 1890. Taken from West Looe it shows trading schooners alongside and the fishing luggers at anchor in the bay. Below: The mouth of the river after the road to Hannafore was built. The area is known locally as "Pennyland" from the charge for the ferry across.

The mouth of the river entrance to Looe. In the top photograph, taken about 1890, the coast road to Hannafore has not been built. The lower picture, taken from the banjo pier dates from 1905 and the photographer was one of a band of early enthusiasts who recorded much of the Cornish scene at the turn of the century.

INTRODUCTION

Early in the 13th century, King John granted licences to merchants of Boyonne in France to fish for whales, conger and hake from St. Michael's Mount up the Channel to Dartmouth, Devon, in return for which the French brought salt and materials for net making. This arrangement brought great prosperity to Devon and Cornwall, so much so that in Tudor times fishing had assumed a position of national importance.

In the reign of Queen Elizabeth the First, certain regulations were laid down. In 1588 it was ordered that of all pilchards taken into Cawsand Bay one third should go to Cawsand and the remainder be sold at Plymouth, Millbrook and other places. This led to complications as the people of Cawsand had other ideas for it was more profitable to salt down the fish in their own cellars, cure it then pack it and export to other countries themselves. This breach of the regulations made the Elizabethan government so angry that a further order was made that "all shadds and Pentises called linns that had been erected since 1588 should forthwith be plucked down". However it also stated that if the required two parts of the fish had not found a ready sale at Plymouth after four tides had passed it could be carried away by water to sell in any other place within the counties of Devon and Cornwall but not overseas. The sales of fish were also stimulated in this country by a Government order that no less than 153 days of the year were to be observed as meatless.

At this time Cornwall had a sea going population of approximately 2,000 men, this number being exceeded only by Devon with 2,800 engaged in fishing. The two counties had more men in this industry at the time than the whole of the east coast ports with Norfolk and Suffolk having about 2,800 engaged in fishing between them. In fact at this time the North Sea herring industry had not commenced but our Westcountry fishermen were already going farther afield. Early in the 17th century Cornishmen were exploiting the Irish grounds and it is recorded that at one time no less than 250 boats from the Mounts Bay and St. Ives areas were fishing for herring in the Irish seas. Following this our boats went to the North Sea and with the Dutch pioneered the herring industry there as it was several years before the East Coast drifter fleets were built up. Our men were not using large boats, very few exceeded 50 ft., but they were a tough race and there are many stories of vessels being caught in gales while making passage home from the North Sea and many never made it.

Men of the smaller ports and coves were prepared to do other things besides fishing. In bad seasons smuggling became a very important and lucrative way of life to inshore fishermen particularly along the south coast. In the 1770's there were 469,000 gallons of brandy smuggled in with a considered revenue loss of £100,000, also 3,500 lbs. of tea smuggled ashore with a revenue loss of £50,000. No wonder there were so many cellars beneath the houses and hidden cupboards. Duties were put on imported salt and also on English salt used for curing pilchards. People were rationed with only 2 lb. to cure a thousand fish which was hardly enough to keep a family for one winter. English salt duty was 3/4d. and foreign 6/8d. which made it very difficult for ordinary people to buy. When it became impossible to afford, the women packers at the factory would strap small bags to their legs or body to take home for their own use in salting pilchards for the family.

In 1785 there were 180 Cornish drifters and 140 seiners all engaged catching pilchards but the seining was a very short season and soon died out. This latter method was carried out by three boats which involved many men. With the very short season the practical fishermen could not afford the expensive nets so there were boat owners, seine net owners and the fishermen all having a share from the catch. It became known as the rich man's fishing. There was deep resentment against the drifter fleet by the seine owners in the 17th century and this resulted in legislation being drawn up to prohibit the use of drift, trammel and stream nets. Throughout the years fishing fortunes fluctuated and during the various wars the foreign markets were completely cut off. During 1812/1813 pilchards were being caught in large quantities and with little sales were being used by farmers as manure.

As has been stated a very large number of Cornish fishing boats were, until these last few years, of the inshore type under 50 ft. in length and it is still true to say that 80-90% of the Cornish boats are small. There is no doubt that fishing was built up with boats using the little harbours and coves around our coastline whereas the larger ports were not used and there were perhaps many reasons for this. There were many small places where a small boat could land so where fishing communities lived they had their boats built to suit their local conditions either to launch from a beach or be accommodated in the shallow waters of a small harbour. This enabled men to fish as it were from their own doorstep. While larger ports like Falmouth or Fowey were not in great use smaller places such as Cawsand Bay, Looe, Polperro and Mevagissey were some of the harbours intensively used by fishermen.

Looe harbour is difficult to get into at certain states of the tide such as on the ebb with little wind or blowing offshore. It was the practice in such conditions, when the fisher folk knew that the boats were coming in, for them to gather at the outer end of the banjo pier even in the night. The craft approaching would throw a rope that was

Vessels waiting for the tide to go up river. At certain states it is possible to wade across.

Building the banjo pier at Looe in 1897.

not too heavy but which would be very long perhaps up to 80 fathoms. The end of the rope was hoisted high up the fore mast while at the shore end all the hands would lay along its length and haul the vessel up the river while the rope being high up would clear all obstacles. The luggers had moorings laid outside the harbour, each boat had its own also a small boat. This enabled the crew to put the small craft on the moorings when going fishing and if when they returned the tide was not suitable for the lugger to enter harbour they could go ashore in the small boat and leave the large vessel on the moorings until conditions were right to bring her in. The small auxiliary boats were used by the young lads of fishing families for fun and games were they not required on the moorings.

It is on record that in 1845 the Looe Harbour Commissioners were established to improve facilities within the port for handling the large volume of traffic using the canal constructed down the valley to Looe and the tremendous increase in copper and tin mining in the Caradon district. In 1860 railway lines were laid to the town and new quays were built at East Looe extending southwards. At this time there were eight Marine Pilots registered with Trinity House at work in the port with four attached to West Looe and the others at East Looe. In the same year as the railway arrived there was at one period a pile up of £4,000 worth of copper ore awaiting shipment on the quay with thirty vessels loading and unloading in the port. Up to the first Great War Looe was still a very busy harbour with many sailing traders coming and going plus the fishing activities. The railway lines were extended down the quays through the centre of a granite works and round the corner to what is now a block of flats and a library. Another line ran from close to the bridge down to the fish market and trucks would be shunted down to be loaded, mostly with long line fish, and during the late afternoon they would be joined up at Liskeard to a London bound train for sale in markets up country. Vessels were loading china clay and copper from Moorswater while others lay alongside the granite works loading this stone which had been shaped perhaps for bridge building, dock construction or large buildings in the cities. Loads of coal were also brought in for the mines. When it was known that ships were coming in local men would go out in small boats to meet them and secure the contract from the skipper for unloading the vessel when she docked. Some of the craft using the port were owned by Looe people while others were often crewed from the port.

Some of the larger buildings stored grain, others timber or coal and there were several used to accommodate crews. The first street up from the quay at the southern end of East Looe was known as Lower Street but the local folk always referred to it as Lodging House Street. Large numbers of men were often staying there while either leaving or about to join ships. Most of those houses are now stores. There was another smaller building in that street which was the cooperage. Men worked there with specially shaped knives and other tools making the barrels which were used for packing the cured pilchards. Many thousands of these casks were made in different sizes and, apart from those used locally, were sent to fish ports in other parts of the country.

The very long building high above the bridge on the side of the hill at West Looe was built as the Coastguard Station and outside on an area of flat ground was a large flagpole or mast used for hoisting signals or ceremonial flags. The Coastguard Officer had his living quarters and an office on the left hand side of the building while the remainder, to the right was occupied by the station personnel and their families. There were at least eight coastguards in residence and their duties were to keep day and night watch on all craft entering or leaving the port and also all vessels passing up or down outside. A particularly intensive watch was kept in bad weather. Communication was kept between the various coastguard stations along the coast and, of course, still is. A seaward observation post was situated at Hannafore and another at Church End, East Looe. There was another flagpole outside the East Looe sub-station and it was possible for the various positions to pass messages to each other by means of code flags from the masts. There was always a very friendly atmosphere between the coastguards and the fishermen and we knew that if we were caught out at sea in bad weather or in any difficulties that they would be on the lookout and would soon react to any sign of trouble.

As the commercial trade in the port dwindled there was no need to maintain a large staff or buildings and the headquarters were sold many years ago. The number of full time coastguards has been very much reduced but with the help of volunteers and part timers a good service is still maintained. The old lifeboat station at East Looe has now become a cafe and store but an inshore life saving craft is available and is kept very active during the summer months. The service is still very much needed for the protection of many people who put out to sea with little or no knowledge of seamanship or respect for the sea and for others who find themselves perched on cliff faces or cut off by the tide.

The very much more up to date equipment both ashore and on board, particularly wireless, which we did not have, enables the coastguards and the fishermen to be in touch at all times. This also applies to coastal and deep water shipping and rescue work of any nature and the splendid cooperation which now exists between coastguards, lifeboats and the service helicopters.

Looking across the river to West Looe about 1914. Fishing boats are alongside and nets are being dried. The large coastguards headquarters can be seen high on the hill.

The barquetine Waterwitch, *built at Pool in 1871, was the last of her rig to sail under the British flag. She is here seen leaving Looe in 1933, loaded with clay.*

The quay at East Looe in 1905. The schooners Priscilla *and* Mary *are berthed alongside and railway trucks are laden with coal for the mines.*

The 3-masted schooner Jane Banks *unloading coal and loading china clay. On the quayside astern can be seen a stack of blocks of granite awaiting shipment. Alongside is visible the stern of a newly built Looe lugger* Dorothy.

Two-masted schooner Lady of Avenal *changing sails while alongside. In the last century this ship was reputed to have been engaged in the slave trade.*

The German vessel Alpha *unloading salt in 1929. This is believed to have been the largest craft ever to enter the port.*

The Scandinavian vessel Nathalia *alongside at Looe, loaded with salt to be used for curing pilchards.*

CHILDHOOD MEMORIES AND ESCAPADES.

I was born in the busy little Cornish seaport of Looe on April 11th 1906, only tipping the scales at four and a half pounds, a fact that was later to cause my mother some difficulty with the family insurance. My brother, Bertie, was born in the same house some seven years later and he grew up to join the Royal Navy, eventually rising the the rank of Captain R.N. My sister, Bessie Peace, followed after another seven years and was so named because her arrival co-incided with Peace Celebrations Day 1920.

At the time of my birth the Pengelly family had been fishing the English Channel for more than two hundred years, but before that, so the story goes, they had been farmers who were introduced to the business of fishing by accident. A few crab pots washed up on the beach excited their curiosity and they decided to try the art for themselves. The success of that venture led them away from the land to the waters from which, to this day, the family still make their livelihood.

We lived down in the town at East Looe, in Lower Chapel Street, the surface of which was cobble stones in many different colours. After heavy showers it looked lovely and clean and making a picture as they shone in the sunlight. It was not, however, so well for youngsters to run around on, as they would trip on the uneven surface and many a bruised and skinned knee would follow. Eventually the street was resurfaced with concrete and then became known as "Cement Street". It was cleaner it's true, but it lost much of its character.

Our home was on the left as one walked down the narrow lane towards the quay and today the house is called 'Tyrina'. There is one front door and inside of this is a pair of further doors which allow two families to live separately but under one roof. Our portion was on the right with one living room on the ground floor, at the rear of which there was a scullery and toilet. On the first floor there was just one bedroom but it had stairs leading to another above which had a 'chicket' window set in the roof. The living room had a coal fired range so that cooking and eating took place in the same room, while lighting was supplied by a double burner paraffin lamp. When we went to bed it was by candlelight, and on very cold nights the bed was warmed by a screw-top stone jar filled with hot water. For some indoor entertainment, my father bought an 'His Master's Voice' gramophone, which had a long horn and played tubular shaped records. This was really something and many hours on a winter's night friends would be in with us listening to the wonders of this machine.

Passing through our street, from Church End towards Buller Street, on the left is a cottage named 'Tolva' which is Cornish for Custom House and on the deeds of the property is the entry – "known as the Custom House". There is a large store at ground level and above this is the present living room which was probably originally used as an office. With a little stretch of the imagination one can see the kegs of spirit taken from some smuggler lining the walls of the store. In this house, during my childhood, lived Alfred Tambling, the Looe Town Crier, a well-known character, who with his wife, reared a large family in 'Tolva' cottage and one of their daughters still lives there. In those days the streets were lit by gas lamps and for some reason their care was the job of the Town Crier. Every evening he could be seen, carrying a long pole with a lighter wick at the end, as he moved from lamp to lamp and again in the mornings he was going through the streets turning them out, a most dedicated man.

At the end of the street on the left is a large building on the top floor of which grain was stored. Each sack had to be hoisted to the top and even today a large iron pulley can be seen fixed to the base of the outside wall. At one time a rope was fed around this and carried through to another some fifteen feet above, over the entrance to the store. The sacks were attached to one end and slowly hoisted upwards, with a horse supplying the power at ground level. The bottom floor of the building was used for stabling the horses which were cared for by one man.

The bakeries in those days were known as 'Bake Houses'. There were two in Buller Street and each had a very large oven built inside into the thick wall of the house. For their heating, men would go up into the woods to cut down branches of trees, chop off the small twigs and shoots and bundle these into 'faggots' of wood. Small boats would be manned on the high tide and taken up river to the nearest point where the fine wood was piled. It was then loaded, brought down river, landed on the quay and stored for use in the ovens. This operation was carried out in the Autumn or early Spring, when there were no leaves on the trees. The dried faggots were placed in the oven and lit. When the heat was considered sufficient, the fine ashes were raked out and then bread, cakes or anything that required baking was put on a long handled shovel. This method of cooking was taken advantage of by many people living nearby and it was common practice for women to prepare a roast dinner, put a piece of white paper on top with their name, and carry it along to the Bake House in the morning to have it made ready for dinner. One of the family would go along at the given time to collect it, ready cooked, for the meal. Many other dishes went into these ovens at different times. There were the famous Cornish saffron cakes that our mothers made, but I dare not mention the ingredients in case I leave something out. All the mixing was done in the evenings, placed in a large bowl,

A very young Alfred John Pengelly with his father and mother.

A group of Looe fishermen at the turn of the century. L to R (rear): Edgar Toms, John Edward Pengelly (my father), George Woodrow Pengelly. (front): Walter Toms, Alf Soady, Leo Prynn.

well covered with cloths or towels, rested on a chair and put close to the dining room fire before we went to bed. This would keep it warm and allow the yeast to ferment and swell the mixture, but if a draught of air penetrated the mix it would be ruined for baking. In the morning it was separated into cake tins and taken along to the Bake House.

The equally famous Cornish pasties were also cooked there. There are many different ingredients used in making a pasty, depending on the cook's wishes or the requirements of those waiting for the 'finished product'. The only 'real' pasty as far as we were concerned was the one made by our mother with a well rolled, flat, round shaped piece of pastry and well filled with finely chopped beef, potatoes, turnip and onion with salt and pepper to taste. When all these items were mixed and laid across the middle, the two opposite edges of the pastry were brought together over the top. The contents had been arranged with the largest portion in the centre, tapering off towards each end to give the correct shape. Starting from one end the crimping operation was begun by lightly squeezing the two edges of the pastry with the forefinger and thumb of one hand and gradually moving along the top while, with the other hand turning down the fold towards you. When completed it looked like a seam. With the pasty pointed at both ends and swelling broadly in the centre it was now ready for cooking, the time depending on the cooker used but a rough guide would be about an hour in a moderately hot oven.

Another favourite dish was potted pilchards, which was much prepared in the summer months, when the fish were in season and oily. The pilchards were headed, gutted, cleaned and placed in a clome (earthenware) or enamel baking dish, sprinkled with salt and pepper plus a little cochineal for colouring and to help soften the bones. A few bay leaves were added to the dish soaked in vinegar with a sheet of brown paper tied round on top to keep the steam inside for cooking and flavour. The dish was taken to the Bake House towards the end of the day, when everything else had been cooked and, together with others, would be put in the oven and left cooking slowly all night. Early in the morning, out would come the dishes of potted pilchards, after which the oven was cleaned and made ready for another day's cooking. These Bake Houses were a blessing to mothers with young families, where for a copper or two much of the baking was done without having to watch over coal stoves at home, especially during the summer months. There were no fancy foods then, no tinned fruits, it was dried fruit soaked overnight and stewed on Sundays. Luxury foods we never missed, not being used to them, but we survived on whatever was available.

There was no delivery of milk or cream in East Looe on a Sunday. During the weekdays delivery was made by horse and cart from the farms, the milk churns with fitted tops standing on the back of the cart. On a Sunday morning, it was the job for the youngsters to fetch this produce for their mothers. This was not at the end of the street but was some distance out in the country and I used to go, with many of the other boys, to Kellow Farm, which was a mile or two over the hill from East Looe towards Millandreath. It took us all the morning and by the time we got back, I am afraid the amount of milk and cream purchased had shrunk considerably and many excuses had to be made as to what happened in transit.

Most of the fishing community lived closely together in the lower part of the town. There was real inter-family life because everyone knew the others troubles and during sickness or bad fishing seasons (and there were many) there was always someone ready to help. There was no unemployment pay or social security benefits, so if we did not earn we had to go without, and at a very early age we were taught to save when we had the chance, spend only when necessary to help tide over the bad times. Many was the time when the generous hearted Mrs. Mutton, of the grocery store, passed goods over the counter to our mothers not knowing when she would be paid, but sure however, that the money would be forthcoming as soon as things improved. To augment the food supply and to ensure there was something to eat, the women would salt pilchards in earthenware jars during the fishing season to use later when required. In the off season, the men would work on plots of land allotted to them by the Vicar of St. Martin's Church. This ground was referred to as 'The Colonies' and it was good for us youngsters to go there with our fathers to help clear the ground and plant potatoes. When grown they were dug up and stored for use in the future, so there was always a meal of boiled potatoes and pilchards to be had when meat was financially out of reach for many days in the week.

There were certain 'friendly societies' such as the 'Racobites' and 'Foresters'. The former was a strictly teetotal organisation, and to become a member it was necessary to sign the pledge of abstinence. As it was possible to join at an early age in the juvenile section, my parents were anxious to have me enrolled, but because of my poor physical condition the Society thought that I would be a liability and I was not accepted. The object, of course, was that in return for a weekly sum the insured was entitled to claim benefit during sickness and on death, the family would receive a sum of money. On occasions a popular event was a march by the Society to church or chapel. All the Racobites assembled at the Sea Front End and, led by a band, off they went to Service but, as I was not a member I would only go along by accompanying my grandfather. Over their shoulder and across their chest, the members all wore a large cream silk sash which was emblazoned on the front with the Society's motto.

My home, the house "Tyrina", from a drawing by John Robbilliard.

The Town Crier and lamplighter Alfred Tambling.

Old Looe Fishermen. (Top) l to r. Back Row: James Pearce, Tom Pengelly, 'Uncle' Fishley, John Edward Pengelly (my father), Jim Pengelly, Jack Crapp, Bill Pengelly, Harry Pengelly, Ben Faulkner, Joe Fletcher, Edmund Pearn, Billy Hill, Bill Martin, Charlie Toms, Jim Toms, Thomas Toms, boy in centre, Edwin Pengelly. Front row: Bill Moor, Jack Pengelly, Tommy Toms, Jack Pengelly (my great grandfather), Jim Mcready, Alfred Pengelly (my grandfather holding dog Dash), Tommy Toms, William Collings. Lower Photograph: Tommy Toms, Sam Organ, Climo, Capt, Salt, Fred Soady, Harry Toms, Bob Prynn, Ben Menhenick, Jim Toms, Bill Southern.

Pilchard Processing. A pilchard store with screw presses compressing the fish in the barrels. The screws are turned a little each day then released and topped up with more fish and the operation repeated.
Below: A processing team, l to r: A dipper with net to lift out cured fish for washing. Next a cooper finishing a completed barrel. Two ladies with final fish layers and a fish washer with his basket. The man used the shovel for putting fish and salt in the tanks for curing.

As children we had to cater for our own amusements. It was not much use asking for pocket money — many times living itself was hard enough. Still, we had fun, perhaps sailing small cork boats that we had made and sometimes at night our pranks even made the policeman chase us around the town. We made trolleys from a plank of wood with a box nailed on top to the base of which we added two axles and four wheels from an old perambulator. The front axle was pivoted so that the boy in charge was able to steer with a length of rope fixed to the axle just inside each wheel. By heaving on either line he was able to turn or by a steady strain on both he could keep a reasonably straight course. A second boy rode at the back and when racing down hills he acted as a brake with his legs dangling and feet dragging. Sometimes the friction of boots on the ground proved too much and when the feet got hot, up would come the legs and the trolley would gather speed, very often capsizing at the bottom of the hill with cart and boys in a painful heap.

When the apples were ripe in the orchards, 'visits' were arranged by some of the lads, and it was one way of getting fruit at times when it was financially impossible to buy it. Always of course, a knitted frock jersey was worn with a length of cord secured around the waist, thus sealing off the bottom and each boy would drop the apples down the neck of the jersey where there was plenty of room. At times there were some very peculiarly shaped boys returning home with their spoils!

One of our escapades stands out in my mind vividly. It was late in the evening and a net had been stretched across the end of a narrow street when the youngsters around the other end started chasing the cats, of which there were many. As the animals got caught in the net pandemonium broke loose with the cats screeching and the owners coming out into the street to find them enmeshed, although some had shot right through as it was a very old piece of light pilchard net. The incident was reported to the police and the next day our grapevine informed us that the local bobby was on our track. When we saw the honourable gentleman the next evening, it seemed he meant business. Feeling very guilty we ran to the sea front where the small boats were stored upside down and we climbed up inside resting on the seats like roosters. It was not long however, before the long arm of the law came under the boat and grabbed the nearest boy. We all came out in turn, were rounded up, and given a stern lecture on behaviour to domestic animals and we promised, shamefaced, not to do it again. No harm came to the cats and the incident ended, but in fact we had a high regard for Constable James who was a kindly man and I am sure understood that we had to let off steam at times, so long as it was not destructive or harmful. Often we would go aboard the vessels that lay alongside the quay unloading coal or loading china clay and if we found a friendly cook we would leave the ship munching ship's biscuits, which were very nice if your teeth stood up to them!

The area of ground at the sea front, known as Church End, was a football ground for the East Looe boys. It was always recognised as a recreation area and many days after school or at holiday times it was used intensively for football. Many pairs of shoes were worn out on the hard ground, trousers torn and bruises gathered on limbs and body. We were sometimes afraid to go home and report what had happened, at the end of a rough match on the sea front, but it is true to say that the game was learnt there. Many afternoons, when the fishermen were waiting to go to sea, their time was taken up playing football at Church End. For years, Looe had one of the best teams in Cornwall, and there is no doubt that many of the local team were taught in the hard school of that pitch. The boys who lived over the river at West Looe went up to the high ground on the downs for their recreation.

There were several annual events that we looked forward to, one of which was the fair on the quay, with all the things that went with it, including swing boats, roundabouts, sideshows and boxing booths. Over at West Looe, the swing boats were placed on the quay edge beside the river and the story is told how an uncle of mine and his pal were standing up in one of the boats in an endeavour to see just how high they could swing. Uncle Fred was the inside man, facing the river, and finally it was swung so high that the iron rods which supported the boat struck the crossbar at the top. Fred was flung out and into the river, but he swam to East Looe, changed his clothes and soon returned to his pals at the fair.

Another great date was Guy Fawkes, known to us as Bonfire Night, and this involved a lot of preparation on both sides of Looe several weeks being spent gathering material for the event. The West Looe boys would drag their stuff up to the downs above their side of the town and build their pile for burning, while at East Looe all the material would be set up on the old battery site at East Cliff. Our lads would collect old discarded fish nets, furniture, tree branches, papers; in fact, anything that would burn. A dummy representing Guy Fawkes was made and trundled around the town on a trolley or barrow to draw people's attention to the event and to collect money to buy the paraffin to help light the fire. One man was always in charge of setting up the heap including the Guy on top fixed to a pole. On the night many of us would have paper lanterns with a candle stuck in the middle, which more often than not caught fire. Early on, some of the lads would get a turnip, dig out the inside, bore a hole or two in the sides and then put their candle inside and these seemed to last a bit longer than the paper variety. When darkness fell, the bonfire was lit and gallons of tar and old oil had been thrown over it which helped it along no end.

The fishing fleet of sailing luggers.
Above: Preparing to leave harbour.
Right: Moving out into the river.

The fire could be seen for many miles out at sea and it signalled the start of the winter fishing season for many years.

Our Christmas depended on the success of the season's fishing — there was no Social Security — but the time was still the highlight of the year. Expensive presents were not on with us but, if times allowed, there was always a little something from Mum and Dad. The selection of presents in those days was very much limited compared with the staggering amount of things available in the toy shops today, but there is no doubt that Christmas was enjoyed just as much with the things we had. Most of the decoration we had to provide ourselves and we were out in the wood looking for the best holly bush, full of berries, to cut just before the festive season. The boys would be collecting chestnuts and storing them for roasting over the open fire on a coal shovel and they would also be gathering logs for the fire. Both boys and girls would be making coloured paper chains for the decorations and there would be a few shiny balls to hang on a tree. On Christmas Eve the stockings were hung up for Father Christmas to call and in the morning there was sure to be a few nuts, an apple, orange and some sweets tucked inside. Most fathers would hang up a stocking as well, just for the fun of it, and invariably next morning it would contain some potatoes, an onion and one or two other small items of garden produce. Many weeks before Christmas our mothers would make the puddings, mixing all the flour, fruit and other ingredients in a large bowl. When the mixture was complete it was split up into portions which were tied up in cloths shaped like small footballs. These were placed into large saucepans and boiled for hours in water and when cooked they were taken out, drained and hung with a cord on a line strung along the kitchen ceiling where they were left hanging until required. The Christmas dinners were prepared and then taken down to the Bake House for cooking. The local shops only catered for the needs of the time and where there are now gift shops, in my childhood they were the butchers, the grocers, the ships chandlers and other necessities for a fishing village and the sailing vessels which used the port.

In the summer it was everyone on the beach and into the sea swimming. Sometimes our mothers took the washed laundry and spread it on the shingle bank or on the hillside to dry and we would be given the job of looking after it. Very few people used the beach at that time but if a visitor wanted a swim there were a few bathing huts on wheels which they could hire, in which to change their clothes. Holidays were for the better off people and only a few hotels catered for those who had the time and money to spend.

When the luggers were in harbour, much of our time was spent in racing the small boats that each had for its own use. We made sails of corn sacks, etc., and raced up and down the river. Sometimes our fathers would take us out to sea on the luggers for a night's fishing. I always remember, when I was very young, standing on the inside end of the pier and throwing stones at my father's boat, as it was being pulled through the harbour entrance, because he would not take me to sea on that day. During the summer months most of the luggers were drifting for pilchards through the night. In the morning the fish were collected from the boats, and then salted down in concrete tanks to be left for weeks curing in the brine. After this process the pilchards were taken out as required, washed in baskets and then passed to the women employed to pack them in barrels. All the fish were packed in layers, nose towards the side, tails towards the middle or centre of the barrel. To make the layer quite level three or four fish would be laid on, all the tails in the centre. When the barrel was packed to the brim, large screw presses were used with a heavy wood base that fitted snugly into the top. This was then screwed down on the fish, forcing them flat and squeezing the oil out at the bottom where it ran into a small channel. This passed through to a concrete tank where at intervals it was collected, put into barrels and then sent to soap factories. The pilchards were laid flat on their sides with the back of one fish just overlapping the belly of the next and it was a beautiful sight to see them when packed and pressed looking rather like a silver flower. When after many pressings, with more layers added, the barrel was full, a cover was then put on and sealed. The end of the cask were then marked with a stencil and black paint stating the name of the firm that processed it and the place where it had to go, which was generally to Genoa in Italy. The fish that had been cured and packed in the smaller Cornish ports was transported to a larger one, usually Newlyn, from where it was shipped overseas. This trade was by far the most important asset to the Cornish Fishing Industry for many years.

Boatmen also undertook other jobs when fishing was bad. Some were engaged to supply sand to builders. Boats were taken up river to be grounded at low water on the sand banks and there they were loaded. As the tide came in the craft were refloated and rowed down river where they were tied alongside the quay just below the bridge. Each boatman then unloaded his sand in a pile and we youngsters often found live sand eels in the heaps which came in useful for bait. As the tide ran out the banks on the upper reaches were washed by fresh water streams which made the sand very good for building purposes and it was used extensively in the old days.

Another sideline was gathering seaweed. This was collected at low tide from beaches and rocks and boats would come in to the quays piled high like a hayrick in fact there have been known occasions when craft sank. At high tide they rowed up river to Sandplace on the East Looe or Watergate on the West Looe where it was unloaded onto farmers' carts to be used as manure on the fields.

With no motors the sailing luggers had to use oars to leave the harbour against a headwind or in a flat calm.

The fleet sails off to the fishing grounds.

22

The fishing lugger, Sweet Home *under way.*

The fleet, having returned to harbour, the job of landing has begun.

MACKEREL'S UP!

Some of the fishing families owned mackerel seine boats. These very long craft of more than 30 ft. in length and approximately 6 ft. beam carried an encircling net a quarter of a mile long, and some 50-60 ft. deep. The top of the net, or head-rope, was extensively corked to float it on the surface of the water; whereas the bottom, known as the foot-rope, was leaded to weight the net down to its fullest extent. A length along the centre of the seine was of a smaller mesh known as the 'bunt'. The seine was stowed in the after part of the boat, just in front of the helmsman with the foot-rope on the foreside, the head-rope on the aft side, and the whole net piled up like a small hayrick. The boat was rowed by a crew of six men, with one other man standing in front of the piled net whose job it was to shoot the net foot-rope into the water when ordered. The helmsman in turn was to shoot the head-rope and also to steer the boat to encircle the shoal of mackerel. Both men had to work in close harmony in shooting the net, to ensure that it did not get fouled as it went over the side of the boat and thus endanger the whole fishing operation. As the boat was moving ahead, the whole net, except the head-rope, was sinking down to form a wall of net around the shoal of fish.

There was another smaller boat, known as the 'Volyer' or follower, about 18 ft. in length which also took part in the fishing operation. It's job was to drop an anchor to moor the larger boat when the net was being hauled on board, which was known as 'tucking the seine'. The smaller boat was also used to dip the fish out from the net in the final stages and carry the mackerel to the fish market for sale.

The seine net mackerel season was a summer fishing. The fish would come close inshore, so close indeed that the shoals of fish were easily seen from the sea-front at Looe. Anyone up on the cliffs could look down and see the concentrations of fish playing on the surface, and at a distance, looking as if strong pockets of wind were striking the surface of the water.

At such times, when the fish were seen close inshore, a cry would go through the Town — "Mackerel's up" and the crews would make a bee-line for their boats. The older fishermen would man the seine boat while the small boat crews consisted mainly of school boys — especially at holiday times — with an older man in charge. One fisherman who was known as the 'huer', was left on shore, and his was the job of going up to the top of the cliff, perhaps in one of the fields where he could best be seen by the boats' crews from the sea and there he would hold a coat or any garment that was easily visible, and he would search with binoculars for a shoal of mackerel. When his particular boat got clear of the harbour and in view, ready for fishing, he would run in the direction he wanted the boat to go, waving his coat also in that direction. This gave the boat's crew an indication where the shoal of fish had been located. Sometimes, however, when the seine boat arrived on the scene, the shoal of fish had sunk below the surface, and then it was a waiting game to see where it would again appear. If it did, the skipper had to determine at what distance he had to commence shooting the net so as to encircle the shoal, and more important, to determine in which direction it was moving so as to also shoot the net in front of it to head it off. Once decided, the shooting operation would commence, with the crew rowing madly, but with rhythm. First a large cork buoy with a length of rope attached to the end of the net went over the side, this end being known as the 'wing' or 'slive'. As the net was being shot and the skipper was steering the boat around the shoal, the smaller boat had picked up the cork float and hove to, waiting to pass it to the seine boat when the circle of net was completed. When this job was done and the seine boat had both ends of the net on board, the 'Volyer' went a short distance away in the opposite direction from the net and dropped a heavy anchor known as the 'tucking grape'. A rope that had been made fast to the anchor was passed back on board the seine boat and there made fast amidships so the boat was secured.

Being anchored, the crew were able to pull on the ends of the net, one end at the bow of the boat, the other at the stern, with the anchor holding the boat against the pull of the net. So the seine was slowly being hauled in with some of the lads on board from the smaller boat, by this time, to lend a hand. Their job was to work what was known as the 'Minices', a hewn granite stone shaped like a bell, 5 to 6 pounds in weight, with a metal ring at the top to which a length of rope was attached. Each lad had one of these, and each in quick succession crashed it into the water by the side of the boat, letting it run down a few fathoms and then up again. To give it momentum, it was swung over the top of one's shoulder, then down into the water. This operation was carried out to frighten the fish back into the bunt or far end of the seine and to prevent the shoal of fish from escaping under the bottom of the boat. The skipper would shout "Down minices, boys". At last the leaded foot of the net would be drawn on board and there was no further need for the minices.

The shout of "Up hooks" meant that the net left in the water was of a basin shape that allowed no escape. With the bottom of the net on board the seine boat, it was now the job of the 'Volyer' to go around opposite the seine boat to lift the head-rope out of the water. So, with the bunt of the seine hanging down between them, the two craft were kept apart by some of the crew with oars placed against each boat. The remaining net was then gradually drawn on board the larger boat and this was known as 'drying up the net'. It became more shallow in depth at each pull until the shoal was now in a confined area of the bunt. The next part of the operation was to get the fish on board the 'Volyer'. Two fishermen fully clad in oilskins and sea boots would take a fish basket known as a 'Mawn', dip it down over the side of the boat into the mass of struggling fish, lift and tip them as fast as they could into the boat, and this process continued until the catch was safely boarded. Sometimes the seine boat and a third boat was used as well to carry the fish in a big haul. They then returned to harbour to land the catch for sale, while the seine boat men would clear away the net and stow it ready for the next shoot.

All this, of course, was great fun for us youngsters, and at the end of the week we were paid a little for our work. This payment was known as 'stocker' to the fishermen, and to this present day, small amounts of fish that may be sold clear of the main catch sale are known as 'stocker', and shared only among the crew.

There was always a joke about the sharing of mackerel seine money, bearing in mind, of course, that the money then in use was in coinage. It was said that the owner of the boat threw it at the top of an upright ladder and the money that pitched and rested on the rungs was the crew's share, while all the money that fell to the ground belonged to the owner!

The crew of the mackerel seine boat Reindeer *preparing to go to sea. The year is 1897 and note the stiff white collars worn by the boys.*

The crew of the seiner Dizzy *tucking the seine. On the port side near the stern can be seen the anchor rope or tucking warp which is holding the boat in position. In the background another seiner* Teddy Bear *is piled with her net waiting to shoot.*

Seine boat Forester *tucking the seine net. A lad in the middle of the boat can be seen swinging the Minice down into the water.*

The volyer, or follower, alongside the seine boat Dizzy, *dipping out the mackerel. Men can be seen with a basket ready to dip into the seething mass of fish.*

Crew of the Dizzy *holding up the net with mackerel enmeshed.*

I START MY SEAFARING CAREER – ASHORE!

At the outbreak of the First World War, my father who was attached to the Royal Naval Reserve, was called up for service. It was on a Sunday morning that the call went through the town for all reserve men to assemble at the Coastguard Station, Church End, East Looe. I remember sitting on my father's kit bag waiting for the men to be off. In the afternoon with a band leading the procession, more than a hundred fishermen from Looe and Polperro marched to the station to entrain for the Naval Barracks, Devonport. It was an impressive sight even for us youngsters.

During the early part of the War, our family moved to Devonport where my mother kept home for my great uncle, a widower, who was coxswain of the Admiral's barge at Mount Wise. It was also very much better for my father to come home on night leave from the Royal Naval Barracks.

Living away from Looe did not please me at all. I missed the boats and the beach and all my school pals; still, I did make friends in Devonport and also we had one or two cinemas and the theatres. Food rationing was very strict and ration coupons had to be handed over the counter at the grocery stores. Sometimes one had to queue for hours to get tea, sugar, butter, etc., at the Maypole shop in Fore Street, Devonport. Many Saturday mornings it was my job to line up at the market place for a long time to be handed 1½ lb. of potatoes for Mother, my small brother Bertie and myself for Sunday dinner.

One outstanding memory was the funeral procession through Devonport of the late Miss Agnes Weston, that great lady who had done so much for Royal Naval personnel in building and staffing the Royal Sailors Rest, to sleep and cater for hundreds of naval ratings for many years. In was a full naval funeral, with Admirals, Captains and anyone who represented the top in Naval welfare attending, and of course naval ratings drawing the gun carriage. There were masses of floral tributes to pay an inspiring homage and say goodbye to a wonderful person. Her spirit lives on in a new building, the old one being bombed out in the Second World War.

After the 1914-1918 war, my father was demobbed and our family returned to Looe, where father took skipper of my grandfather's boat *Sweet Home.* The fishing was seasonal, which meant that at certain times of the year the boats would be engaged in fishing for different kinds of fish. This is where the inshore fishermen must learn various methods according to each season, unlike the deep sea fisherman who perhaps does the same kind of fishing all his life. So the pattern at that time was – in the spring of the year from March until the end of July, long lining; during the remainder of the summer until the end of September, drifting with pilchard nets at Newlyn, and during the winter it was to return to our home port for a season fishing. At first this was for pilchards and mackerel with drift nets, then early December the Bigbury Bay herring season would commence and continue until February.

On the 11th of April 1920, having reached the age of 14 years, my school days were over. Like many other boys of my own age I was looking forward to going to sea and becoming a fisherman. In Looe, with a fleet of 45 fishing luggers and many other smaller boats, nearly all of which belonged to fishing families, it was the thing to do. I joined my father, who was still skipper of the *Sweet Home,* and my first fishing was long lining, mainly at night. The first job was to catch pilchards for bait with drift nets. When the bait was secured it was all out steaming to the fishing grounds, during which time the crew would cut up the bait into small portions and bait all the hooks, approximately two thousand. The long line was about three miles in length when laid on the sea bed and this gear had to be hauled by hand. When fishing for conger, ray, skate or ling, the lines were laid during dark hours as this was the best time to catch these species. It happened sometimes that the boat had to fish all night with drift nets to catch enough bait and the only thing to do then was to steam off to the fishing ground and wait all day until the next evening and then shoot the lines with the sun going down. The end of the long line is weighted to moor it on to the sea bed, to stop it from being swept along with the tide. A line was also attached, long enough to reach to the surface, with a float and marker dhan with a flag on top, to denote where the long line was. The long line was then laid with the tide, in a fairly straight line. When half the line was laid a second dhan was attached, then another when the last end was laid. It was then the job to clean up the decks, have a good meal and prepare to pull the lines back on board. It was usual to wait until the tide turned in the opposite direction, and this could help to lift the line and thus make it easier to pull aboard. If all went well, the fishing trip would take about 24 hours. The main grounds for long line fishing at that time were off the Lizard, to deep outside the Eddystone and sometimes up to 45 miles from it. After a few years, with larger boats, more engine power and a motorised long line hauler, very much more fishing gear was used.

It so happened, however, that I was a very seasick young man. It mattered little if the weather was fine or rough, every trip to sea I was sick. In fact I well remember one day, knowing the weather was not good outside, I had to go below deck in harbour and be sick. After three months with no improvement, Father said, "You will never make a fisherman". I was, of course, bitterly disappointed at this, accepting, however, that he knew best. I left the boat and became a shipwright's apprentice with Mr. Frank Curtis and Mr. Larny Mitchell, who were joint partners in a boat building business at Polean, West Looe. The building was a very large wooden shed, which originally had been used as a hut for living quarters on an army camp. Soon after the First World War, with the soldiers being demobbed and sent home, there was no further use for such buildings. Built in sections that could easily be taken apart and rebuilt at any other suitable place, these large huts were offered cheaply and were bought and used by many small business people to further their work. Curtis and Mitchell were trained boat builders and all they needed were the right premises but the huts were at a camp some miles away. They had to be dismantled, transported to Polean and re-erected down in the valley behind the south facing hill. In that part of the valley there was no sunshine during the winter months and it became very cold after frosty nights, with no interior heating, just a large draughty building which made one feel, in the cold of winter, that the prisoners in Dartmoor had much more comfort. The toilet was outside the building in a small tin hut about four feet square and at the back, inside, it had a wooden bar across, some four inches square, as a seat. There was no comfort there either, so there was no justification for wasting time. We were, however, a happy team together. There were two bosses, one a fully trained shipwright, Mr. Jack Hocking and four apprentices all about the same age, George Hoskin, Gerald Toms, Spencer Northcott and myself; also Larny Mitchell's very large brown dog, Jim. At crib time he could be seen looking anxiously for the scraps of food, but judging by his size, however, he was well fed.

My wages were two shillings and sixpence per week for the first twelve months but the second year I was to receive five shillings a week. One of my first jobs was to saw frames out of large oak planks with a handsaw, for a lugger called the *Eileen* which the firm was building. The wood was very wet as the large oak logs used had been soaking in the river for months before going to the saw mills at West Looe above the bridge.

Fishing in general improved considerably from pre-war years. So much had the palagic stock increased in fact, that many times during the winter fishing, some of our luggers were unable to take on board the many very heavy catches of fish enmeshed in their fleet of drift nets. At such times, to ensure the safety of boats and crews, some nets had to be cut adrift full of fish to be lost on most occasions for all time. This was a costly affair and it became apparent to many boat owners that bigger craft were required.

In 1921 my Grandfather decided to have a large boat built, of forty-four feet six inches overall length, thirteen feet six inches in beam with a draught of more than six feet. It was to be a boat with a most unusual name. The unique choice derived from the fact that two other luggers in the Pengelly family were already called *Our Boys* and *Our Girls,* after the children. Grandfather was determined that he should not be forgotten, and in October of that year, the lugger *Our Daddy* was launched and fitted out with two Kelvin engines, one thirteen horsepower, the other seven horsepower, installed in an engine room aft, with a cabin behind it, fitted with five sleeping berths and a coal fired cooking stove. She was built by Mr. Richard Pearce and his son, with their staff of shipwrights at the boatyard at West Looe end of the bridge, where the Ice Cream factory now stands. Close by was a saw mill where all the oak timber was cut to make the keels and framing for the boats. The large circular saw was operated by two brothers, Bill and Tom Pape. Their job was to winch up long lengths of oak trees that had been left in the water to season and place them onto the saw bed — a long metal table that carried the timber to the saw for cutting into its required length. This was at times quite a formidable job. The two brothers, however, were experts at their work, and a very great help to the boat builders in the Looe area. In those days builders could choose the wood they required for the job and it was nothing but the best.

I had already made up my mind that I was once again going to sea and had no intention of being shut in a boat building yard. How could I resist going out in such a fine boat, so I joined *Our Daddy* in 1921 for the winter fishing. Mr father was skipper, his brother Ernest was the engineer while two other men formed the crew and I was appointed cook. It was three years later before I was able to go to sea without feeling sick and perhaps it was helped by my taking charge of a new and recently installed engine.

For a few years the seasons came and went following very much the same pattern in the fishing except that more craft entered the industry. In the early thirties boats used line up to seven miles in length with more than 6,000 hooks attached and with larger boats going deeper and further into the English Channel it became impossible to lay all the long line in the dark hours. So it had to be that part of the line was laid in the daylight hours and one very important factor emerged from this. It was that in laying more line in daylight, boats were catching some turbot which was an almost unknown fish to us through fishing in the dark hours. So it became more profitable to us during May, June and July to wait until full daylight in order to fish almost entirely for turbot, and this practice was carried on through the years. The very real problem in fishing with long line in the English Channel was the fact that having laid such a long length of fishing gear on to the sea bed, other fishing craft such as trawlers would often tow their gear across the line and cut it away. In the early days it was the sailing beam trawlers that were the culprits.

As fishing progressed, however, with motor and steam power it gradually became a hazard to fish with long line out in the Channel particularly on a clean sandy bottom, where the trawlers could operate. On laying the line

Clearing the long line on Our Daddy *in 1944.*

Right: The local children have a sea trip with the lugger flag bedecked including the Cornish Cross of St. Piran.

we were never sure that we could get it safely back on board and many times some gear would be lost. French trawlers were mostly to blame for this, they seemed to swarm into the Channel at times. In these early days one of the great drawbacks in the fishing industry at the smaller ports was the marketing of the catch, as buyers could pay what they had a mind to.

Although there were auction sales, this meant very little as they would get together and agree prices then share out the landed catches. The only fish weighed was conger and ling, while thorn back rays were sold at so much per dozen. If you received £1 per dozen from the buyer you were lucky. Turbot were sold at so much each and if the fishermen were paid two shillings and sixpence for each fish, again they were lucky.

As the summer months came along, the demand for fresh fish declined. There was little or no refrigeration and fishermen were informed by the buyers that the longline fish had to be landed at the fish market at a certain time to catch the train in the afternoon. This meant that when the tides were not suitable for the boats to get into harbour early enough to land fish, arrangements had to be made to have hand carts out on the banjo pier. The big boats being at anchor in the bay, smaller boats would be loaded with fish, then rowed into the pier where each crew would have to carry the fish up the pier steps and on the the hand carts, then drag the carts of fish up to the fish market. This operation had to be repeated several times with a good catch of fish and all this on a hot day after being at sea for twenty-four hours could be very tiring and frustrating. Also, of course, people were turning to other foods and fruit, so that at such times it was a lower price to the fishermen. Towards the end of July men were glad to give up long line fishing when the gear was put on shore and into the stores. Men would then get busy cleaning up and painting the boats, then take on board a fleet of drift nets for the pilchard fishing season.

At this time there were no pilchards to be caught off the South East coast of Cornwall and the summer season took place at Newlyn, fishing off the Mounts Bay and the Wolf Rock area. So on a Monday morning, with the boats freshly painted up, looking like yachts, they would be taken by the crews to join the West Country pilchard fleet for fresh fields of fortune.

I shall never forget the first night fishing in Mounts Bay. We joined with boats from St. Ives, Newlyn, Mousehole, Porthleven and Mevagissey — there seemed to be hundreds of lights from all the boats for miles around. It was a most impressive sight, like a town afloat. In the early morning most of this large fleet would be landing their catch to the buyers at an agreed price which lasted very often throughout the season. The fish were collected in baskets, transported to the curing stores by horse and cart or by small boats to be salted down in concrete tanks, as already mentioned. The fishermen had to count the fish into the baskets, picking up six fish with both hands, counting from one up to twenty-one every time six fish were dropped into the basket. This was known as the long hundred. Every hundred fish, so called, was in fact 126 fish. The twenty six fish over the hundred were taken in case of damaged fish. Each basket would hold two hundred, five baskets were a thousand, ten thousand were known as a last. Payment was worked out by so much per thousand.

With the number of Looe boats fishing at Newlyn there were several lads of my own age, so there was plenty of company and we made many friends with the lads on the boats from other ports and of course the local boys. No fishing for pilchards on Saturday or Sunday, and the fact that very often we were not able to afford the fare to go home for the weekend by rail, gave us time to look around Penzance, with its shopping centre and one or two cinemas.

Newlyn was always full of craft of all shapes and sizes with trawlers, long liners, all the drifter fleets and also when the spring tides were on, a fleet of French crabbers would come into the harbour or anchor just outside. These were all sailing craft manned by the Breton fishermen, a very hardy race of seamen whose staple diet seemed to be bread and wine with an occasional stew-up of fish. It was no problem to barter some pilchards or mackerel with the Frenchmen for a crab or two or a bottle of Vino if one wanted it. At evening time if the tide was in the harbour, there was good sport to be had catching silver bream with a line over the stern of the boat whilst moored to the quay. One thing that used to startle us when trying to get some sleep on board in daytime, was the fact that the huge stone quarry nearby would at certain times of each day send off a series of explosive charges, blasting the rock from the face of the cliffs. The noise was shattering at times.

One very great asset to us at Newlyn was the Mission to Deep Sea Fishermen. The Superintendent and staff always made us welcome and many hours were spent in the building. There was plenty of hot water to wash and shave, tea and cakes and a good game of billiards. It was home from home to us youngsters. Mrs. Badcock kept the grocery store and bakery, where our boats at Newlyn bought their bread and other foods. Pasties were ordered during the week, once or twice as a change of diet and very large pasties sold for a shilling each. We used to call them 'train wreckers', a very good meal, however. Every Friday, when her lad Edward came down to the boats with their orders, the kindly old lady sent a specially made cake of saffron or madeira to give to each boat's crew. She affectionately became known to us lads as Mother Badcock.

Our Daddy fishing at night

painting by E. E. Turner.

CAUGHT IN WOLF ROCK

It was towards the end of the summer pilchard fishing season at Newlyn, with the shoals of fish beginning to move to the Westward, following the usual pattern in the migration of the pilchards at that time of year. The fleet of drifters leaving Newlyn harbour in the late afternoon were steaming to fishing grounds to the north-west of the Wolf Rock Lighthouse, and in the boat *Our Daddy,* we were one of the last boats to leave. Later, as the fishing boats were taking up positions to shoot their nets, my father, who was the skipper decided to stop short of the fleet, so we were the nearest boat to the Lighthouse at that time. It was a lovely fine evening, with a very light northerly wind and, having shot the nets, the crew then set about cleaning out the net room into which a few pilchards had fallen when hauling the nets the previous night. So they had to be picked up and the hold scrubbed out all ready for the next haul, and then it was tea-time, which we had on deck. It was noticed at this time that we seemed to be drifting with the tide, towards the Wolf Rock. The daylight was beginning to fade, the light on the lighthouse was flashing in an arc, it was time to decide what to do. There was more than one mile of drift nets in a line from our boat, it would be more than two hours working as fast as we could to retrieve all that length of gear. Father gave word to pull the nets on board, the engine was started up, the crew all dressed in seaboots and oilskin frocks, started the long haul. It was not possible to unmesh any fish that were in the nets, they had to be bundled into the net room, nets and fish. Within an hour we had come close to the lighthouse and it looked as if we were drifting directly towards it. At the end of the second hour of hauling, our boat had drifted in so near that the flashing light was up above us. The situation was getting critical, should we have to cut our remaining nets away to save ourselves and the boat, or should we drift close past the lighthouse and be safe? We had little time to wait and see, the dhan light attached to the end net suddenly went out; drifters always used a dhan with a light attached to show in which direction the fleet of nets were in case any craft cut through the gear at night. The man hauling the head rope shouted, we were caught, the net had come fast in the rocks or buoy of Wolf Rock, the fully extended depth of the net was approximately 62 ft. All hands were hanging on to the net, in seconds, however, the head rope had parted and the net ripped through from top to bottom. Our boat had drifted out on the west side of Wolf Rock, we had left one net and the dhan entangled in the rocks. It was a near thing for us and our boat, we could only thank God that we were safe. The net lost was an old one, it was always the practice to use the newest nets close to the boat with older nets towards the pole end, or farthest end from the boat. Whatever the lighthouse keepers were thinking when they saw us in under the lighthouse, working nets, is anyone's guess, but we were thankful to be on our way back to harbour.

At the end of September the season ended and it was then that the Looe fleet would leave for home. The drift nets were dipped in hot cutch, a substance taken from the bark of a certain type of tree grown in Burma, which was like hard pitch and had to be boiled in water in a concrete tank. When the cutch dissolved in the water it looked like drinking chocolate. The pilchard nets were dipped into this hot mixture to preserve the cotton fibre that the nets were made of and this process had to be repeated every five to six weeks, when the boats were fishing with this type of gear. Towards the end of October, boats were made ready for the winter drift net fishing. Nets were taken on board that had a larger mesh size so as to be able to catch pilchards, mackerel and herrings which were found to be shoaled together early in the season. For many years fishing would commence on the 5th November and it seemed as if the fish knew the date. This mixed fishing was followed up until around the 12th December when the Bigbury herring season commenced. Already many of the Cornish boats had joined in the winter fishing which was based at Plymouth.

More than 100 boats of all sizes from Cornish ports and, before Christmas, a fleet of steam drifters from Lowestoft and Yarmouth would join in the fishing, sometimes up to 80 large vessels. All these craft would fish the herring shoals which were to be found off Plymouth and east of Eddystone and Bigbury Bay where most of the West Country boats fished. East coast fish salesmen came down to Plymouth to sell the catches of these steam drifters. Many fish buyers also came to the port, also Scottish women to pack the herring into barrels who were experts at the job. After a good night's fishing, Sutton Harbour would be crammed with craft of all sizes, taking it in turn to land their fish. In the early morning each skipper took a certain amount of herring from his catch in a basket on to the quay as a sample of quality. The salesmen would then offer in turn this particular boat's catch for sale by the cran. This was approximately 28 stone, or four 7 stone baskets full in measure. Each salesman had his allotted stand on the fish quay for selling. The Cornish boats had their own salesman. The many buyers from all over the country created a great demand for the good quality herring.

A fine 'portrait' of the lugger Our Daddy *taken from the banjo pier as she leaves harbour.*

A peaceful scene with the luggers Our Daddy *and* Eileen *in port with oil skins drying.*

Our Daddy *puts out to sea in the teeth of a strong south easterly wind and a rolling sea. To keep her steady the mizzen is set aft.*

Early one morning, towards the end of a very tiring week of fishing, the boat skippers took their herring samples as usual on to the quay to await sales. The skipper of the Looe lugger, *Lead Me,* Jack Jago, a big heavy man, took up his sample to await his turn and sat on an upturned barrel to rest. Jack was known to be a very sound sleeper — and it was not long before this proved to be the case, as he fell asleep with his basket of herrings by his side. After some time, his crew became anxious about his non-return to the boat and one of them searched and found Jack fast asleep sitting on the barrel, while the herrings and the basket had vanished, much to the shameful enjoyment of the many fishermen around. Old Jack, however, was as big hearted as his physical build and took it all in good part.

It may be of interest at this part of the story to try and explain how nature helped our fishermen to find the fish without any electronic aids. Most of the know-how was, of course, handed down from our fathers and older fishermen. As I have already stated the fishing is seasonal and I start with the long lining.

There were certain areas of the sea bed where very small fish live and in turn the larger species will be there at times to feed on these smaller varieties. It depends largely on the nature of the seabed itself what fish you will find, whether it be rocky, shingle or sandy or muddy. You often find conger, ling, cod or pollock feeding on the little fish living on a rocky or rough sea bed and in the many wrecks strewn along the sea bed. In turn, flat fish like turbot, plaice, brill, lemon sole, demersel fish, are more often found on the sandy or soft sea bed where sand eels and worm live. Having to rely in the main on migratory fish in this part of the English Channel, each is to be found more plentifully in its season of each year. Some areas of the sea bed have no life whatever on them, just barren areas on which no good fishing is obtained, so the sea bed, in fact, is very much like the land, where certain areas or fields will or will not grow certain kinds of crops.

The fisherman, like the farmer, has a very much better prospect of success in his profession if he is aware of these areas and so avoids doing the wrong thing. Both the farmer and the fisherman have to rely very much on nature to do its share. The very great difference is that the farmer can till the land and eventually see the crops grow, the fisherman has to rely entirely on nature to provide the fish, at least up to now and the very real danger to fishing is that in applying science to finding and catching more fish, the fishing grounds have been seriously depleted and in some parts of the world where intensive industrial fishing for palagic fish has taken place stocks have become so low as not to be economical. "Palagic" fish such as pilchards, mackerel and herring are also seasonal fish, swimming mostly up in the water, off the sea bed and, therefore, the drift net or the midwater trawl is used to catch these fish. The movement and temperature of tidal current has much to do with this sort of fishing. The various kinds of plankton or feed coming to certain areas off the coast or close inshore at times will bring the fish with it for its natural food. During the winter season this plankton will become very compact, heavily concentrated and the pilchard and mackerel too, will shoal up into heavy bunches with the feed.

In the early days fishermen had to look for signs of fish. It was not uncommon to see one or two large whales feeding on the shoals of fish, lifting their heads to the surface and blowing the oily spume that looked like escaping steam from a hole in the top of their heads. When the whale went under for another mouthful of fish, it would leave a large oily patch on the water. This could be smelt for quite some distance, if it was on the windward side. Sea birds would be hovering overhead, waiting to swoop on an injured fish that often would rise to the surface. Gannets would be diving on the fish. These wonderful birds with a wing-span of some six feet would be flying along looking down into the water to find a silvery fish for its prey; sometimes flying fairly low and at other times very high up in the air, depending on the fish being at a certain depth under the surface. If the fish were swimming deeply as was often the case during summer time or under certain weather conditions, particularly the pilchards, the deeper the fish the higher the gannet would fly. On sighting, the bird would dive like an arrow, folding its wings just before plunging into the water, and I have seen gannets meshed in drift nets 50 ft. under the surface. Boats would try and shoot the nets where the gannets were diving before the dark hours as it very often proved that a heavy concentration of fish was there. Palagic fish will sense the weather change very often before the fishermen know it. Often at such times, the shoals of fish would swim very much faster, creating a turbulance on the surface like the broiling of a tide rip. Also at times on a calm day, looking down into the surface of the water, a mass of tiny air bubbles would be seen rising to the surface, just as if it was coming out of a ginger beer bottle. At times this would be seen over large areas, another indication that the shoals of fish were in fast swim and in the way that fish breathe they were creating these air bubbles. It often happened that after a particularly heavy night of fishing with the drifter fleet, very bad weather would quickly follow. Fishermen would say that the fish had felt the change, meaning of course, the weather conditions.

There were times during the winter drift net fishing that boats would have to fish throughout the night. When looking for fish at night, the deck lights were put out; with only a small mast headlight on, and navigation lights almost blocked out — just enough to be safe from other craft. Some of the crew would place themselves on deck close to the bow, looking down over the side into the water as the boat moved forward, while the sea, on a fairly clear night, would look as if it had millions of little stars. In very clear water this phosphorescence would give off a strong luminous effect, thus fish could be clearly seen darting through the water. When going through a shoal of fish at night, an iron weight was used to thump the deck. The fish would seem to light up the boat like a large silver wave under the bow; this was known as brimming. It was the skipper's job to turn the boat around, then the crew would shoot the nets with a following wind, all lights blazing on deck. The object was to shoot the nets into the water as fast as possible into the shoal of fish. It was always important in drift net fishing off our Cornish coast to shoot the nets if possible in the twilight particularly if the weather had been fine and the sea water was clear. In the daylight the fish would see the drift net under these conditions, but when the light began to change to dark, fish seemed to rise nearer to the surface and, being unable to see the net, would become enmeshed. This was more noticeable during the summer pilchard fishing. Very often the longer the twilight hours the better the fish would swim into the net and for a longer period. At times of overcast skies with the light failing rapidly, the fishing period would be very much shorter. At such times as this, in the dark, the net would show up like a long silver wall under the surface and this would drive the fish away from it. It is the belief of the fishermen that during the changing light the vision of the fish is impaired for a time so as not to be able to see the net and there are times when the only fish caught is at this period of time.

Another way of finding fish at night in fine weather was to listen for them. When it was known that shoals of fish were around, engines would be stopped and when all was quiet, men would cup a hand to each ear and listen intently. It often happened that the fish were up to the surface playing around leaping out of the water. A shoal of fish could be heard hundreds of yards away. This method was often used after gales of wind when the water was sanded and no brimming was possible. There are so many changes in the movement of the palagic fish owing to weather conditions, tidal movement, moon effects, that no man can predetermine fishing. It is always a challenge to determine the time of operation or try to, and then act accordingly. This is what makes fishing so fascinating, unlike any other calling.

Fishermen engaged in drift net or hand line fishing for palagic fish would look for the colour of the sea water, which was caused by changes in the plankton, indicating the feed of certain fish. In the spring of the year, March or April, the sea water off the south east Cornish coast becomes jet black, altering to this almost overnight. It was common at this time of the year for fishermen to come in from a trip to sea, perhaps crabbing or trawling and remark that the black water had come, thus giving the drifter men the idea that the pilchards had arrived.

In the mackerel season we would be looking for thick green water, again the plankton would be so concentrated as to effect the colour of the sea. During the winter herring season the water would very often be a milky colour. During the Bigbury herring fishing we would be looking for this light colour. It was a spawning area and it was understood that the herring which carried the melt would give out its fertilising liquid, and the herring with the egg roe would spawn afterwards, thus allowing the roe to become fertile. During this period, the herring would lay on the sea bed until the spawning was completed. The ultimate failure of this fishing was blamed on the trawlers who fished for herrings during the spawning period when the fish were laying on the sea bed, thus also destroying the spawn itself.

It is true to say that although the pilchards shoal during the winter season, in the summer months these concentrations of fish break up and spread out. This, in effect, means that while the mid-water trawl is highly successful during the winter in catching pilchards, it has not as yet superseded the drift net during the summer months; this is perhaps because the fish are spread out thinly in the sea and also that in the clearer water at night with all its luminous effect, fish are frightened away from the trawl before they can be caught.

With the change over at Brixham and Plymouth from sailing trawlers to steam and motor vessels, plus the very great increase in the number of large French trawlers that were able to fish into our three mile limit, the grounds were being over-fished. During the winter months the stocks of pilchard, herring and mackerel, were being seriously depleted by these large French trawlers. It became so bad after the mid-twenties, that many of the younger fishermen were forced to leave the industry during the summer months to accept jobs on yachts as deck hands and some as skippers. So the way of life for many of us was fishing during the winter at home, then during March leave home to join yachts for the summer season. This included cruising yachts and for some, the largest racing yachts afloat at that time.

The fifteen metre yacht Paula.

YACHTING

It was in the Spring of 1927 that I received a telegram from Bill Butters asking me to join the yacht *Paula* at Burnham-on-Crouch. I was nineteen years of age at that time, so off I went by train, after saying goodbye to my family and girl friend. On arriving at Burnham in the evening, I learned that the yacht was stuck on the mud a long way down the river Crouch. It appeared that in trying to beat up river against a head wind, the ship had sailed too close inshore, and a channel had to be cut through the mudbank to allow her to float into deep water as the tide came in. The owner, Mr. Perry, and his wife were on board at the time. The skipper was Archie Cole, with Jack Grimwade as mate (both from Burnham-on-Crouch), while old Bobby George was cook-steward, with Bill Butters and myself as crew, all three from Looe.

Paula was a fifteen metre yacht built for racing. As there were few ships left of this class we had to race with different size craft, such as the *Moonbeam, Sumurun,* etc. This meant that according to the size of craft, a handicap would be arranged of so many minutes in time for or against each vessel sailing in the race. Most of our racing took place inside the Isle of Wight. Several weeks before our racing season commenced were spent at Burnham-on-Crouch anchored in the river so that the skipper and mate were able to have each night at home. It was very pleasant at Burnham and several times on a Sunday, Bill and I had tea with the mate and his family in their home, and often we went to the Chapel with the skipper and his family. It was all a new experience for me being away on a yacht. Sometimes we went up the Ipswich River to anchor at Pin Mill, a lovely little spot where the Thames barges would refit and clean up, also a light drink was to be had in the Butt and Oyster Inn close to the yard.

Early one morning, whilst anchored at Burnham, we were scrubbing down the decks. I looked away up the river and saw what looked like a huge hayrick coming down with the tide. As it came closer it was seen to be a London barge loaded with hay which seemed to be stacked half way up the mast. One of the crew was standing on top of the hay directing the skipper who was navigating the craft down river between the yachts at anchor. Only the topsail was set on the barge. It was a wonderful sight to see how a two man crew would handle these London barges and beat to windward in a breeze, but better still was to witness the annual barge race at Southend. Tremendous pride was taken in these grand old ladies of the sea, both by owners and crew and no doubt tales are still being told of those races in the London river area.

Towards the end of my first summer season in the racing yachts I developed a back strain commonly known as lumbago, so it meant that I had to return home for rest and treatment. During the off season period of 1927, with several other young fishermen, I journeyed to Fowey and enlisted in the Royal Naval Reserve. This involved six week's training at Devonport, two weeks square bashing and four weeks in a destroyer including drill parade, rifle drill, gunnery training and marching about with new boots on rough ground which took the skin off my feet, so I ended up after the first week peeling potatoes in the cook house. When this initial training was over we were split up to serve in destroyers. We had, of course, been put into classes with many more new entrants like ourselves, so with several other lads including my own pals from home, I joined *H.M.S. Saumarez* for a few trips to sea.

One day, in the morning, the ship was laying alongside the dockyard wall, when the working party, including myself, were ordered to wash paintwork on the outside hull of the ship. Planks were lowered over the side and I happened to be on one with a pal of mine called Dick Stephens from Looe and we were both dressed in white duck suits which was the working rig. The ship's bow was pointing up stream, with a moderate head wind blowing down stream. Dick and I were about two-thirds of the way back the length of the vessel. The coal-fired galley was over under the bridge, and it must have been an opportune time for the cook to clean the galley flues, which he did. Having filled a large bucket with soot he promptly made a bee-line for the side of the ship, then tipped the contents over quickly without looking and Dick and I got the lot. There were never two better looking "Black and White Minstrels", but the show was enjoyed by all and we joined in the laugh as well.

It was fortunate for me that having a fishing boat in the family, with my father as skipper, I was able to come and go as I pleased, so it was back to the winter fishing. Again the season was very grim, very little was earned and with no unemployment benefit or no social security it was inevitable that by the following March we were looking forward to going away yachting to earn more money.

It was in early March, 1928, when I received a letter from Captain Ted Heard of Tollesbury, offering me a berth aboard a brand new twenty-one metre racing yacht *Astra,* which was being built for Sir Mortimer Singer. This ship was a Bermudan cutter approximately 100 ft. long and of 164 tons with a mast 130 ft. high. She was being built at Gosport and was to carry a crew of 18 men. I promptly accepted the job, with two others from Looe, Bill Butters and Joe Uglow, and we joined her at Camper and Nicholson, Gosport before she was launched. It was a wonderful experience for me to become a member of the crew of such a lovely craft, the first of two of this large class that were not gaffed rig. The other, named *Cambria,* was built on the Clyde, and her skipper, Alfred Diaper hailed from Southampton.

Astra *racing inside the Isle of Wight, reefed down in a fresh wind. An unfortunate accident occurred just after this shot was taken.* Astra *was using a brand new suit of sails with the mainsail stretched which allowed the boom to drop lower than usual. Mr. Perry was standing in the main companionway with his head above the hatch watching events. When the ship was put about on the other tack the low boom swept across the companionway and crushed Mr. Perry's face in the hatch cover. As we were near the finishing line at Calshot,* Astra *sailed right on to Southampton where the injured man was transferred to hospital where he remained for some time before recovering. We were all upset and I had served with him on* Paula *during the previous summer. It was a hard race which we won.*

All the crew were on board *Astra* as she slipped down the launching way. Unfortunately, however, there were some lumps of iron ballast lying between the launching rails so high that *Astra's* rudder struck them, being damaged so badly, that the next day she had to be slipped to have a new rudder fitted. After a few days she was taken to Portsmouth Dockyard to have the racing mast lowered into place. This operation was carried out with a huge German floating crane which had been taken over after the First World War and it was said that a German engineer was looking after this very large piece of floating equipment.

Then it was back to Gosport and on moorings to continue fitting out. Much more work had to be done, by Camper Nicholson's workmen to get the ship ready for racing, while Ratsey and Lampthorn, sailmakers, were busy getting all the sails ready to set and try out. After a few very hectic weeks of preparation, we had her ready for trials, and by now our crew had got to know one another. Captain Heard and his mate, Mr. Sampson, had made a list of jobs, so that each member of the ship's company knew exactly his work while racing, or at other times. So much of the success in handling the ship when racing depended on team work and for the crew to jump to every order given by the Captain.

Astra's crew was made up mostly of young men brought up in the fishing industry around our coast. Captain Heard and his son, Ted and the mate Mr. Sampson, were from Tollesbury; from West Mersey were second mate Bert French and Arthur Howes, mast headsman; while Harold Stroud and his brother Alfred, caterer, were from Whitstable. Frank Paddy, the bosun hailed from Plymouth and other crew members from Brixham and Southampton. The caterer, Alf Stroud, was a very important man as far as the crew were concerned. It was his job to buy all the food for the crew and we all paid him to pool the cost of living, a matter of eight shillings per week per man in those days. Deck hands wages were £3 per week, less five shillings taken out to ensure good conduct, payable at the end of the season. Each day the ship raced, crew members were awarded £1 for a first prize; fifteen shillings for a second prize and ten shillings for crossing the starting line with no prize. This money was also added up and paid out at the end of the season, so there was a great incentive to stay on for the whole season, like it or not. *Astra*, however, was a happy ship with a very good owner and a skipper who knew his job and was held in the highest esteem by his crew. Captain Heard had previously skippered 12 metre racing yachts that were approximately half the size of the 21 metre class and with a crew of only four men including the skipper. It was a challenge and a great responsibility to race a ship with a crew of 18 men against some of the largest racing yachts afloat, such as *Britannia, Westward, Lulworth, White Heather, Shamrock* and *Cambria*, the new Bermudan cutter. Most of the skippers of these yachts had been handling this type of vessel for many seasons and there was keen rivalry between them when racing. Men like Captain Sycamore of *Shamrock* and Captain Mountfield of *White Heather* knew every trick in the book.

When *Astra* was completed, several weeks were taken up in sailing up and down the Solent, stretching the sails and trying out the different suits to be used according to weather conditions and of course training the crew in handling the ship.

The first racing of the season was in mid-May at Harwich where three days were organised for the big yachts. The first brought a fresh wind and a feeling of expectancy and excitement prevailed amongst our crew. A brand new ship with the Captain and several members of the crew, like myself, racing for the first time in one of the largest Bermudan cutters afloat, after being in very much smaller craft.

The race was the usual 40 mile triangular course; first leg, a run before the wind; second leg, a reach, then a beat back to the windward starting and finishing line. On the last leg home *Astra* was lying second to *Shamrock* both close hauled on the wind, when suddenly every hank attached to the luff rope of the mainsail began to break. These metal hanks, spaced every few feet on the luff rope fitted on a track on the after side of the mast, nearly to the masthead thus allowing the sail to slide up and down on the mast and so remain in position. It was a tricky job getting the mainsail down safely in the fresh wind and this incident put us out of the first race. We were confident, however, that our ship would hold her own with the rest of the fleet under fair conditions, and this was proved in the races that followed. The Bermudan cutters were closer when beating to windward than the gaff rigged vessels and were also faster. Perhaps more important was the fact that the Bermudan mainsail with no gaff and no jack yard topsails to handle ensured easier work for the crew in the general handling of the ship.

After Harwich, where we enjoyed eating shrimps from the fishing boats and whose crews were well known to our crew members from West Mersea and Tollesbury, we moved to Southend and were in two races there. Wherever the big yachts raced, a local man was engaged as Pilot to advise the Captain of shoals, tide movements, winds, etc.

The races to follow took us west to race in the Solent, at Ryde, Cowes and Lymington, where it was very much harder work for the crews in this enclosed waterway. These large craft with their big keels needed fairly deep water and so could only race through the channel between the Isle of Wight and the Solent sand-bank. If the wind

Astra running before the wind with every stitch of canvas set.

Astra. *(Above)* At anchor off Camper & Nicholson's yard at Gosport. *(Right)* Drifting home in light airs at Falmouth.

was straight through, it meant either a run from the starting line to the lee mark and a beat back, or the other way round, first a beat to the weather mark and then a run to finish. Very often, whilst the ship was on a run before the wind, was the only time throughout the day when a sandwich could be hastily eaten by the crew on deck, passed around by the forecastle cook and his mate. Beating to windward meant a series of short tacks every few minutes, so after sailing 40 miles up and down the Solent keenly contesting with the other ships for first position, crews were glad to end the day with a good meal and more often than not a change of dry clothes. This, of course, after stowing the sails, clearing up the decks and washing all the varnish work, such as covering board, companion hatches, and skylights that were of mahogany, with fresh water sponges.

At the height of the racing season, in the Solent, there were several weeks of racing every day except on Sundays, often wearing the duck suits, damp from the previous day's racing. In wet weather there was little chance of really drying clothes properly. Often fingers would split at the side with gripping the hard Italian hemp ropes, so after a few hard days many fingers would be bound up with brown hemp fibre, which helped to heal and avoid any further damage.

To get ready for a day's racing, it was up at 6.30 a.m., a cup of tea, then on deck in bare feet with the crew scrubbing the deck with long handled deck scrubbers. The mate and second mate dipping up buckets of sea water and throwing on to the deck, thus all available hands would carry out this task. Then when well scrubbed, shammy leather cloths were used to dry up the deck as well as possible, clean and polish all brass fittings, uncover the mainsail, put some of the headsails up in stops, i.e. lightly tied around so that when the order was given to break out the headsails, a sharp pull on the sheet of the sail would part the stops allowing the sail to break immediately. At the end of the preparation, it was breakfast at 8.00 a.m. with no more sit down meal to be had until the race was over and the ship squared up at anchor, usually at four or five o'clock in the afternoon.

After having had breakfast, it was get ready to sail, up mainsail, secure the anchor below deck after pulling it up on board with a deck tackle; break out one or two of the headsails as necessary and get the ship sailing round to line up and prepare to cross the starting line with the other ships, at the given time of the race committee.

Each member of the crew was at his appointed position on deck for racing. I was with the bosun Frank Paddy from Plymouth in the after guard looking after the topmast backstays and mainsheet, so except for lending a hand hoisting or lowering spinnaker, most of our work was on the stern of the vessel. Frank was much older than me and we were very good pals, all through, being together for several seasons, which enabled me to learn a lot from him.

After racing in the Solent we left for Ireland to race at Dun Loughaire, in the Irish Republic. When we arrived there and anchored up, we were advised that perhaps it would not be wise to go ashore in the evenings on leave, in order to keep out of any trouble that could arise under certain conditions. We spent only the afternoons on shore having a look around and stretching our legs. We did two races there, then left for Bangor further up the coast in Belfast Lough to complete two more races. It was then set sail for Greenock and the Clyde where *Astra* was put into dry dock for a clean up. This gave us the chance to take a coach trip to Glasgow and an evening at the theatre which was very much enjoyed.

Our first races on the Clyde were at Gourock and Greenock. The weather conditions were very bad, with fresh winds and on the second race, *Astra* started with a reefed mainsail, small jib and staysail. This, however, proved to be too much for our gear, for after rounding the loch close hauled on the port tack, a strong gust of wind struck us and before we had time to look around, the mast snapped off, three feet up from the deck. All the sails and mast were in the sea; the ship had been sailing with the starboard rail underwater, then suddenly swung upright, nearly throwing overboard the crew, who had been lying on the weather side of the deck. The remainder of that day was spent in taking the sails and rigging off the 130 ft. mast in the sea with everything on it, which was quite some job. The mast was a made spar with 64 pieces of wood glued together, flat sided 9 inches across and 18 inches through fore and aft. It proved to be very limp and therefore was not a success. When all was cleared up, arrangements were made to tow *Astra* back to Gosport for a new mast and a new suit of sails etc, but this incident lost us a great many races with the other ships. After a week or two refitting, we re-joined the racing on the South coast.

One day at Torbay, during the first season racing, a fresh westerly wind was blowing. After the race had been in progress for a short while, the large gaff rigged yachts *Britannia, White Heather, Shamrock* and *Lulworth* gave up in the freshening wind, as they were carrying too much sail. This left only the two new Bermudan cutters with *Astra* leading *Cambria*. The competition was so keen between these two skippers, sailing these new craft that neither would give up the race. The *Britannia* tender, a naval minesweeper, followed our two vessels around the course in case we had trouble with our sailing gear. On rounding the seaward mark to race back into Torbay, the wind was abeam; we were forced to lower the staysail because *Astra* was under so much pressure of wind that all the lee deck was under water almost up to the skylights. The owner had to leave the cockpit just in front of the wheel as the sea was lapping in over it. On the after side of the main sheet horse a lifebuoy was lashed in the middle of the deck, but the rush of water was going so hard across the stern deck that the buoy was broken from its lashings and washed overboard.

Astra won the race without mishap, severely trying the gear and crew. On another occasion racing down the Solent towards the western mark, on an almost dead run with spinnakers on the starboard side and the mainsail eased forward on the port side, the yachts had to go around the mark, leaving it on the starboard hand, to come sharply around on the starboard tack to a beat to windward. This exercise meant quickly lowering the spinnaker below, getting the spinnaker boom on deck, pulling the mainsheet in as well as the headsails. All this had to be carried out whilst approaching and rounding the mark buoy. The ship was swung around it very fast with all the crew busy trimming sails and the men working on the fore and after end of the ship had to be careful they were not thrown over the side. On rounding the mark, *Cambria* was very close on *Astra's* port quarter, trying to cut across her stern to come up on her weather quarter. *Cambria* had a short bowsprit, the bobstay of which sliced across *Astra's* stern cutting the flat part of it off with the name and quarter fairleads attached. My mate Frank Paddy saw what was going to happen and shouted to me to jump clear which we promptly did. Luckily, *Cambria's* bowsprit just missed *Astra's* topmast backstays by inches, which would have been disastrous.

This incident put *Cambria* out of the race. In the evening, whilst at anchor in Cowes' roads, Camper and Nicholson, shipwrights, brought back the part of *Astra's* stern that went away hanging from *Cambria's* bobstay and securely fastened it on again. The season continued without further mishap and towards the end of September, it was laying-up time. To lift out the mast, put all the sails and running gear back into storage for the winter, *Astra* was pulled on to a slipway in a cradle, cleaned and painted through below floor, then covered up until the following spring.

I would like now to pay a tribute to the owner of *Astra*, Sir Mortimore Singer, who was a very kind and considerate gentleman. His good lady was French and it was understood that they met when she was a nurse in a hospital where Sir Mortimore was an accident patient from an aeroplane crash. They lived in a large house overlooking Torquay Harbour where many times during the summer *Astra* was berthed. Each week that we were racing, hampers of cakes, etc. were sent on board for the crew from the owner's house and every racing day, each member of the crew was given fruit, paid for by the owner. These extras were very acceptable to the men, whose living standards, although adequate, were by no means luxurious, on eight shillings per week. Perhaps the most generous gesture was the fact that each member of the crew who was prepared to rejoin *Astra* for the following summer season received a retaining fee all winter. I received £1 per week, and on this security and the racing money that I had been able to save, my sweetheart and I were able to furnish a small cottage and be married. The winter fishing was not very good but unfortunately there was little else that many of us could do and to make matters worse the weather conditions were as bad as the fishing itself. I earned ten shillings throughout the first twelve weeks after marriage, so with no social security of any kind, it was a blessing to receive the fee from *Astra's* owner. Under these conditions, it was little wonder that we were anxious to rejoin the yacht in March 1929, to earn a living at least for the summer months.

Many of the former crew rejoined *Astra*, including three of us from Looe, Ned Pengelly, Joe Uglow and myself, all good pals. Joe was assistant cook, while Ned and I were on deck. We had one very likeable character on board, Erny Buttel from Emsworth, bowsprit end man, a very hefty fellow who liked his pints of beer. In the rather cramped crew's quarters down below in the bows, iron-framed cots for sleeping were fastened to the side of the hull, so that it was possible to fold and secure them flat against the side of the ship when not in use. When lowered for use they were suspended with a strap up to the deck beams, at each end on the outside. Erny and I had the two cots, one on each side, right up in the bow, so close as to overlap at the far end, close to the deck. It was my job at night, to lower both my cot and Erny's because he was too large to do it. When all cots were lowered, I would be laying in mine waiting for Erny who would take a dive headlong towards the bow, to land either on his tummy or his back into his cot and I then had to cover him up. We were so close up under deck that Erny could do nothing except lie dead flat. This was an act that all the crew seemed to enjoy watching, when it was turn-in time.

Astra took part in the East coast racing, and then to Ireland. Whilst racing on the Clyde however, we had the sad news that our owner, Sir Mortimore Singer, who had been in hospital a short time, had passed away which was a great shock to all on board. We had lost a friendly owner who always gave a good deal of thought to the well being of his crew. This was in June. We expected that the ship would be laid up and the crew sent home, but we were kept on and the ship remained in commission. No more racing was done, but wherever the big yachts were, *Astra* would be there at anchor. Some of the crew were encouraged to take a turn as extra hands on the other racing vessels so as to earn a little extra racing money. When the racing season ended once more, it was back to Gosport to dismantle all the gear and slip the yacht for the winter, but for us it was away home to the uncertainties of the winter fishing.

Cambria, *close hauled and reefed in a fresh breeze.*

SHAMROCK V.

The winter fishing in 1929 was not good as weather conditions made it almost impossible to fish until near Christmas. It was fortunate for me that our late Sir Mortimore Singer had bequeathed in his will an amount of money for each member of his yacht's crew, according to his period of service and I was sent a cheque for £50 the week before Christmas. This was very acceptable and enabled my wife and me to tide over until the spring. During the winter I received a letter from Captain Heard stating that he was going to take command of Sir Thomas Lipton's new racing yacht *Shamrock V,* that was to race in America for the America's Cup and that I could have a berth on her if I wished, to which I promptly replied, yes. Two more Looe men were taken on as crew members, Joe Uglow, with whom I had already been for two previous yachting seasons and Jack Sargent (Looe's present Harbour Master). Jack and I had been together fishing for several years with my father on board the *Our Daddy,* and I was just twelve months his senior. In those days, however, he was the much better sailor. Keeping clear of being seasick was not my strong point, and it was three years at sea before it thankfully left me able to do my job properly. As teenagers Jack and I decided to take up the smoking habit. Having bought a pipe each, we bought an ounce of tobacco between us, but this we never used up as we found smoking did not appeal to either of us. Both of us remain non-smokers and teetotallers to the present day. We were in one another's company both at sea and on shore, always good friends and here we were now, with another pal from Looe, Joe Uglow, making up a part of the crew of a famous racing yacht.

It was in March 1930, the three of us left Looe to join *Shamrock V* at Gosport, but on arrival we found that the ship was not ready to accommodate the crew, so we were found lodgings on shore for the time being. Jack, Joe and I were put into a small guest house on the front of Gosport near to the shipping yard where Mr. and Mrs. Carter were extremely kind to us, treating us as their own family. Many of *Shamrock's* crew were men who had been with Captain Heard before, in all 22 hands, including the officers. They came from Tollesbury, Wivenhoe, West Mersea, Southampton, Brixham, Plymouth, Port Isaac and Looe. I was offered the extra job of looking after and running the motor launch for which I received an extra five shillings a week. This was used for all sorts of jobs such as taking the caterer ashore in the mornings for food, etc. I was also engaged in running to and from the *Erin,* Sir Thomas Lipton's steam yacht of some 1,400 tons which was his home whilst *Shamrock* was racing. When we were anchored off, I used to take the men ashore in the launch for evening leave and again fetch them later on. If we were laying off Southampton or anywhere close to the home of members of the crew then I would take them ashore in the evenings and collect them again in the mornings so as to give these lucky lads a night at home. Much of the off racing period was spent laying in Southampton waters, so these crew members were more fortunate than those of us who lived in the West Country. The conditions of employment for a crew member were: £3 per week, whilst in British waters, with the normal racing prize money, i.e. £1 first prize, 15 shillings second prize, 10 shillings for a start. On leaving for America wages rose to £5 per week and if we were successful in winning the America's Cup there would be £50 per man, and for sailing the race and not winning, £25 per man. When the races were completed our contract was over and we were to be sent home to England, passage paid.

Shamrock V was a J Class racing yacht, 119 ft. 10 ins. and in addition, a centre board was fitted to slide down through the lead keel a further 9 ft. if required. This lead keel was 80 tons in weight and the ship's total displacement 134 tons. The mast was a built wooden spar 160 ft. in height. The crews quarters were forward with a double tier of metal framed cots on each side that could be folded up against the ship's side when not in use. There was a small galley with two paraffin pressurised stoves and a wash basin for the crew. The Officer's berths were on the afterside of this. The Crew's toilet was very seldom used because it was in the wrong place, next to the Captain's cabin, so a bucket in the after sail cabin was the most convenient. The middle of the ship normally used as a saloon and cabin for the owner, was built in to store places for sails and spare gear as Sir Thomas Lipton lived on board his steam yacht *Erin* wherever *Shamrock* raced. His representative Col. Duncan Neal, joined us only for the racing periods and most the time the whole of the ship was used by the crew. *Erin* was our escort everywhere we sailed and in addition to carrying all *Shamrock's* spare racing gear, in fine weather she would take us in tow to the different ports for racing. In order to get *Shamrock V* and her crew into racing trim, we joined the other big yachts in a series of races at Harwich and Southend and in the five races at these two places *Shamrock* won them all. We competed with *Lulworth, White Heather, Candida* and *Cambria.* Our following races brought us down inside the Isle of Wight to Ryde, Cowes, Lymington, then across to Ireland, at Dun Loughaire, Bangor, where we were presented with a Shamrock plant for luck by the staff of Lipton's Stores who paid us a social visit whilst lying at anchor there. On up to the Clyde for more racing where one day we had King Alfonso of Spain on board, racing with us who was a very keen yachtsman. I remember well when standing on the aft deck close to the skipper, we were racing on a dead run up the Clyde, goose winged, mainsail eased forward, spinnaker squared, King Alfonso looked up the Clyde

Astra *leading the gaff rigged yachts* White Heather *and* Shamrock. *(Predecessor of* Shamrock V*)*.

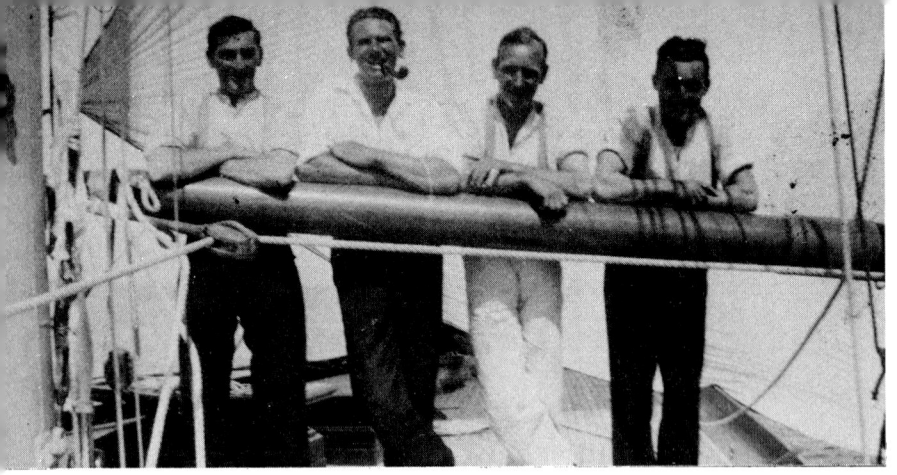

Aboard Shamrock. *L to R: A. J. Pengelly, S. Stroud, B. Bradock, T. Heard (Captain's son).*

Three men from Looe aboard Shamrock. *J. H. Sargeant, J. Uglow, A. J. Pengelly.*

Alfred John Pengelly at the wheel of Shamrock *in Southampton Water.*

Looking aft aboard Shamrock *when crossing the Atlantic with main binnacle amidships.*

towards the Holy Loch and pointing said, "Captain, you will have the wind from there". He could see that the yachts racing further up had the wind in an opposite direction to that which we had. It was not long before we were caught aback with the wind dead ahead. Hastily we had to lower the spinnaker, take in the spinnaker boom, (this boom, by the way, was sixty feet long) bring aft the running gear, main runner stays and back stays, etc. We did not, however, get the mainsheet in fast enough and when the main boom swung in, all the main sheet wrapped itself around the ship's counter stern. It took a long time to clear everything up and get the ship underway, close hauled on the wind.

In all, *Shamrock* took part in twenty-two races with other English vessels and in these she won 14 first prizes, 4 second prizes, giving up twice in bad weather rather than risk straining the gear. In one of these, *Shamrock* had a considerable lead, but the risk to mast and gear however, was too great to carry on. The racing proved that according to English standards we had a fast ship and everyone was looking forward to the America's Cup races.

On the 6th July 1930, *Shamrock V* left Gourock, on the Clyde, in tow with *Erin* to return to Gosport to prepare for the Atlantic crossing, passed the South Rock light vessel at 7.45 p.m. from Ailsa Craig, Codling light vessel at 4.00 a.m. on the 7th, abreast of the Smalls at 1.00 p.m. and the Long Ships was abeam at 11.30 p.m. on the 7th. The weather had been fine and on the 8th we passed the Lizard at 1.30 a.m., Berry Head at 9.00 a.m., arriving at Gosport at 6 p.m. On the 9th, *Shamrock* went into dock at Portsmouth for a clean up and overhaul. The top mast was lifted off from the racing mast leaving 100 ft. of main on which could be set a jib, staysail and a loose fitted trysail on the track on the afterside of the mast. A square yard was also fitted on to the foremast. A mizzen mast was put on board behind the steering wheel. *Shamrock* now became yawl rigged with iron stanchions fitted around the covering board with wire safety rails attached. The only thing to help a man stay on board when racing was a three inch rail on the outside edge of the covering board, so when the ship was listing, one was able to place his foot against it to keep from sliding off the deck. The very low rail, of course, allowed any sea water to run quickly off the deck of the ship when coming upright after having the lee deck underwater when racing in fresh winds. Two life boats were secured on *Shamrock's* deck, all necessary dry provisions were taken on board, but meat and other perishable stores had to be put on board *Erin* and kept in refrigeration to be used when we wanted it. However, only twice during the whole voyage across the Atlantic was it fine enough to transfer any of this food from *Erin*. Our only form of amusement on board was a gramophone with a very limited selection of records. A deep sea navigator was engaged to sail with us and he joined the ship at Gosport a few days before we sailed.

Shamrock V sailed out of Portsmouth Harbour on Saturday 19th July 1930 with all the craft in the port blowing sirens, flags flying everywhere and people cheering as we passed out below — a wonderful send-off. There was great expectation of this ship, the first America's Cup challenger for 10 years. Out in the Solent the ship was swung for compass adjustment, and when completed, *Erin* put a rope on board us, then we were under tow and away. A strong South West wind was blowing and we were forced to anchor just inside the Needles at the Western entrance to the Solent for the night. Our crew had already been split up into two watches, and this meant half of the crew on deck for a four hours duty, the second half of the crew to come on duty for the following four hours until evening. Each half of the crew would then do one two-hour watch, thus changing the times of watch keeping and these are known as the dog watches, i.e. 4 - 6 and 6 - 8.

On Sunday morning at 5.00 a.m. *Shamrock* was again taken in tow and shaped course down Channel, while we set mizzen and jib to keep the ship steady. By the time Start Point was reached, the wind had freshened and being late afternoon it was decided to run back to Brixham and shelter for the night. We dropped anchor in the bay at 6 p.m. by which time it was raining and blowing hard. A government trawler was anchored close to us and her skipper kindly sent over some Sunday newspapers, so the evening was spent reading the news. Our three Brixham crew members, Jack Cempton, Harry German and Bill Bradock, were disappointed at being in sight of home and not being able to go ashore.

I will treat the rest of the voyage as log entries.

Monday 21st   At 5 a.m. we left Brixham under tow with a moderate north west wind and heavy south west swell. We later set reefed trysail, mizzen and jib, slipped the tow rope and shaped course West by South for the Azores as we were taking the southerly route across the Atlantic expecting a fine weather trip which however was not to be. In a few hours the English shores were lost to sight but all hands were in good spirits and hoping for a quick passage across. Down below deck Gracie Fields was singing to us on the gramophone.

Tuesday 22nd   With the wind north and moderate the ship is rolling badly and the crew is busy parcelling and covering all the running gear which was chaffing. We semaphored to *Erin* asking her to take us in tow but she replied that while the breeze held we must sail on. Later, when the wind veered easterly and light she took us in tow and we made good progress all day. In the night it was

	fascinating to see the shoals of pilchards swimming away as the ship moved forward through the phosphorescence in the water which lit up the vessel.
Wednesday 23rd	The morning brought a strong north west wind and *Shamrock* had to be battened down fore and aft. At 10 a.m. a steamer passed us homeward bound and wished us good luck and bon voyage. Towards evening the wind dropped and by midnight it was calm when the hatches were taken off to let fresh air through the ship.
Thursday 24th	The sky altering fast with a strong south west wind quickly whipping up a nasty sea. We were forced to slip the tow and to ease the ship along under reduced sail. As one particularly heavy sea rolled along, *Shamrock* did not rise soon enough and it came in over the bows. Most of it went down the forecastle hatch where it washed the cook and his precious stoves all over the floor. Some very uncomplimentary remarks were shouted up through the hatch from below. On go all hatches again making it very uncomfortable below deck and we have to take our meals amidships sqatting on the floor. It is impossible to sleep below so the watch off duty have to lay in the sail bins amidships to try and get some rest. *Erin* spoke to us at 8 p.m. and gave us some news she had picked up on the wireless. At midnight it was blowing hard with heavy squalls and *Erin* remains jogging along on our port quarter. Shortly after the wind breaks off and we alter course to sail in the changed direction but it would seem that our escort did not notice our move. After another heavy squall we can no longer see her but hope we will make contact again at day light.
Friday 25th	We look for *Erin* in vain but she seems to have vanished like the phantom ship of old. The weather improves and we shape course for the Azores.
Saturday 26th	The wind remained light with fog and these conditions lasted all through the day and night.
Sunday 27th	The fog lifts at midday and we set the bowsprit spinnaker but lowered it later and set the squaresail. With a good following wind excellent progress was made throughout the day and night.
Monday 28th	In a light south east wind we lowered the squaresail and set the jib, staysail and trysail but only made slow progress.
Tuesday 29th	The day dawned with a light wind. Early in the morning we sighted the Azores which pleased everyone on board as the water supply was running low and we had been very careful in its use. On seeing land each man was allowed enough to wash his clothes. It was a fine sunny day and with the amount of washing all the crew had hung around the ship she looked like a Chinese laundry!!
Wednesday 30th	*Shamrock* entered harbour at Fayal at 3 p.m. and there to our surprise was *Erin* lying at anchor. She had arrived at 10 a.m. this same day. She had been searching for us for five days and running short of fuel had put into Fayal for bunkering before continuing the search. They were very relieved indeed to see us enter harbour, as she had been reluctant to wireless home for fear of causing alarm. After we had moored, the starboard watch were allowed ashore for a few hours to stretch their legs and have a look around. It was a very interesting little place mostly inhabited by Portuguese with the women — in bare feet — seemingly doing most of the work. The local cheap wine was rather too strong for our lads and several had the privilege of being escorted back on board by the local Militia!!
Thursday 31st	We spent the day cleaning the ship. *Shamrock* had been strained somewhat during the bad weather and had been leaking for some time which meant pumping out every four hours. This trouble was attended to and put right while stores and fresh water were taken on board, following which the port watch was allowed ashore for two hours. We left Fayal at 5 p.m. in tow with *Erin*, with a long swell but fine and this enabled us to keep up a good speed all through the night.
Friday August 1st	At noon it was very fine with a smooth sea. Shoals of flying fish were darting in and out of the water, like little silver birds, some even landing on deck.
Saturday 2nd	With the wind moderate all day the crew were able to sleep during the watch below and get some rest. At midnight our mate was taken ill and we asked *Erin* for medical aid.
Sunday 3rd	As soon as it was light *Erin* launched a boat and took our mate back on board where the ship's doctor kept him for the remainder of the voyage.
Monday 4th	The sky looks bad and with the wind increasing on go all the hatches again and the skylights are screwed down.
Tuesday 5th	The weather is so bad we are forced to slip the tow and set trysail, mizzen and jib. However, in the evening the conditions improve a little and *Erin* again takes us in tow.

Shamrock V *on passage across the Atlantic. The two top photographs demonstrate the pendulum effect of her racing hull in bad weather. As she rises to one wave her forefoot is uncovered while another roller lifts her stern and pushes the bow under. In the large picture she is bowling along merrily with jib, staysail, trysail and mizzen set.*

Wednesday 6th	At daylight the wind quickly freshens and *Erin* alters four points off course to allow our ship to make better weather of it. The wind is now on the port bow with a heavy sea running. At midnight the wind backs west-south-west and freshens.
Thursday 7th	The day dawns with a strong wind and a nasty sea. If this keeps up we are afraid of losing our mast which looks very shaky in these bad conditions. *Shamrock* is shipping a lot of water but one blessing is the fact that she has no bulwarks so the sea rolls in over, sweeps the deck and is gone over the other side. At midnight a swinging strut stay on the mast is carried away. It took us two hours to repair it in the dark sometimes having to run aft to dodge a heavy sea that broke on board. These racing yachts were built for speed under sail and so finely shaped at each end that when plunging into the sea the bow would go under allowing a lot of water to come aboard. When she did lift forward to a sea the counter stern would push down allowing the sea to come in over each quarter and meet in the middle of the deck aft. With the very heavy keel in the centre of the ship she was like a pendulum with only the middle remaining above water. Under such conditions I would much prefer to be in a fishing boat.
Friday 8th	At 4 a.m. the wind is coming up in squalls with enough rain to knock one flat and there was again no sleep to be had below deck. At 8 a.m. there were more squalls and you cannot look to windward in them or they would cut your face. Everything was wet through below — "someone must have killed a cat". All hands are rather fed up. The flag halyard carries away also the square-sail topping lift. Towards evening the weather moderates a bit but the ship is still rolling badly. By midnight the sea had become smoother and the moon was shining brightly. It was fine — what a contrast!
Saturday 9th	At 4 a.m. we are making good progress with a light north west wind. At 9.30 a.m. *Erin* stopped and sent over some fresh stores with a report that our mate was improving. She also said she was running short of coal and it we get many more strong head winds she will be forced to slip our tow and make for the nearest port to bunker up thereby leaving us to make the best of it. We had a light wind by midday and were running at a steady nine knots. We repaired the port lift and dried out all the wet gear. At 8 p.m. the breeze was making south west and by midnight it was freshening fast and we set reefed staysail.
Sunday 10th	At dawn strong south westerly wind. By noon still strong but not a lot of sea. At 4 p.m. there was only another 490 miles to go and with the wind and sea abeam and weather not looking too bad our spirits rose. We were logging a steady nine knots and if we can keep that up we should make port on Wednesday. At 6 p.m. we lowered the staysail and we were getting a bit fed up and tired of constantly slacking this off. There is no sleep to be had below when battened down and this we have to be with a "hat full of wind". By midnight we are again back with heavy seas and a strong south wester.
Monday 11th	Very bad morning with heavy seas and the ship rolling like a barrel. I have never known a vessel roll like this and it became necessary for each man in turn at the wheel to be lashed to the mizzen mast. We tried to have breakfast below but the plates were sliding all over the floor. The atmosphere is very bad, hot and damp, with everything wet through. Our crew have not been in their quarters in the forecastle for three days and nights, the only man to venture there being the heroic cook who has to sit on the floor to watch his stoves. On many days we have been lucky to have anything cooked at all and great credit is due to our two cooks in trying to arrange any sort of meal in such bad weather conditions. By tea time at 4.30 p.m. we were down to tinned pilchards. As we were opening them a sea breaks on board much of which empties down the skylight overhead and exit pilchards from the tins, washed out. We had a busy time scraping fish off the floor, what a life, fishing on the mess deck.
Tuesday 12th	Light wind all the forenoon, freshening at 4 p.m., again dropping at midnight.
Wednesday 13th	At 4 a.m. it was calm. We made good speed and passed the Nantucket lightship in the early morning. We are getting close to the American coast now and at noon we were being greeted by fast launches from New London. *Shamrock* entered harbour with a strong escort of yachts and government craft with many cameramen taking movies. Well, here we are in America and very glad to be here too. Everybody seems to want *Shamrock* to win the Cup and we will have a jolly good try. We dropped anchor in New London Harbour after a very bad Atlantic crossing with adverse weather conditions which took 26 days.

The crew of Shamrock V. *l to r: (back row) Charlie Dan, cook (Wivenhoe); Tom Cudmore, steward (Tollesbury); Sidney Stroud (Whitstable); Lemman Cranfield, first mate (Tollesbury); Captain Ted Heard (Tollesbury); Bert French, second mate (West Mersea); Alfred Stroud (Whitstable); Cyril Heard (Tollesbury); Chris Hilliard, cook (Wivanhoe). Centre: Jack Sargeant (Looe); Joe Uglow (Looe); Bill Bradock (Brixham); Jack Gempton (Brixham); Billy Wilkinson (Tollesbury); Harry Harman (Whitstable). Front: Dick Howard (West Mersea); Ted Heard, son of the Captain (Tollesbury); Alfred John Pengelly (Looe); Harry German (Brixham); Frank Paddy (Plymouth). The photograph below is of Sir Thomas Lipton's* Erin.

THE AMERICA'S CUP

New London was a naval dockyard town where we were to get the ship back into shape for the cup races. A very large houseboat had been hired for our crew's accommodation while in America and it consisted of two decks. On the lower were our living and sleeping quarters also the galley together with a large generating plant for lighting and power while on the upper level were the stores. The craft was named *Killarney* and all the crew's belongings and bedding were quickly transferred to her. There had, however, a night watch to be kept aboard the now deserted *Shamrock* and after drawing lots it was Frank Paddy and myself whose job it was to remain on board for the first night in harbour.

The next day was spent in getting the ship alongside the dockyard wall and preparing to restep the topmast into the mainmast and then lifting out the mizzen mast and square yard. Many days were spent in making ready the boat but in the evenings we went ashore to the pictures or theatre. Incidentally it was very pleasing to experience the wonderful hospitality extended to us by the American people. Wherever we went, wearing our jerseys with the name of the yacht on the front, we were not allowed to pay for any entertainment.

When the ship was rerigged, with the dockyard help, Captain Heard had the inside of the vessel cleared of all bulkheads etc, and it was then possible to look through the ship below decks from one end to the other – like an empty shell. This was to allow full airspace inside for maximum buoyancy. After nearly three weeks of fitting out we were towed, with our houseboat, to Newport Rhode Island which was a large yachting centre. On our arrival we were again given a good reception by escorting craft and hundreds of people lining the hills at the entrance.

On September 5th at 10.30 a.m. *Shamrock* left Newport for her first day's sail in American waters. We had two men from Ratsy & Lapthorne's on board in case of sail damage. We unbent the No. 1 mainsail and after a good day's sailing we returned to harbour at 5 p.m. The next day we were out again during which we tried out the No. 2 mainsail and returned to port at 4 p.m. On the following day, September 7th, the crew cleaned off and varnished the ship after which we were given the afternoon off, our first spell of leave during the day since we had arrived in America. The next morning *Shamrock* was hauled up on the slip to have her hull cleaned and repainted in the famous green colour which had been brought out from England especially for the job. Before the races were to start the crew were allowed to go ashore at Newport throughout the day on leave, one watch at a time. Many English, Scottish and Irish families were living in the area and several times our lads were invited to the homes of these folk. A luncheon was arranged by the Civic Authority and what a wonderful meal that was with lobster and every other kind of shellfish. All sorts of drinks were in abundance including Scotch and Irish whiskey and one must remember that at this time in America there was officially strict prohibition of alcoholic drinks. Bearing in mind that our crew had seen little strong drink for many weeks it was not surprising that before the luncheon was finished some of our lads were the worse for wear and one at least fell off his chair! Despite the laws it seemed very little could be done to prevent alcohol from entering the country and many times at night we heard the very fast launches coming in from the sea presumably with the stuff on board as the following story bears out.

It was late afternoon and I was mooring up the motor launch alongside the dock quay at Newport when suddenly I heard a familiar voice calling my name. Looking up I saw Bill Southern from my home town who was a shipwright and incidently had helped to build my grandfather's boat *Our Daddy* in 1921. I knew Bill had gone to the United States but I had no idea in which part of that vast country he was working. Getting over my astonishment I said, "What the devil are you doing here, Bill?" He replied, "I am in a better racket than you, Alfred John. I know that all the hands on your yacht are picked men but the mate I work with would pay you better than you have ever made before, even from a top catch at Looe on the *Our Daddy*. Come on", he added, "Pack up for the day and I will take you a trip around the Island". It was fortunate that I had finished work for the day and off I went with Bill. Our first stop was a restaurant named 'The Granite Block' and everyone seemed to know Bill. We had a real tuck in of fried clams and everything else after which we went on to Bill's digs where we met a lot of his American friends. Later on he asked me if I would care to go and have a look at the speedboats on which he was the engineer. He took me to a small out of the way boat yard up the Fall River where I went on board one of his boats. I was at first surprised at what I saw but I soon realised what it was all about. The craft was a large speed boat with three 450 h.p. Liberty engines which gave her a speed of 30 knots. Bill switched on the centre engine and the sudden noise so startled me that I jumped out of the engine room. She was liquor running and was fitted out to carry 50 cases. He told me of one evening, when the fleet was in Newport, he was being chased by a coastguard cutter and

Shamrock V *stretching her canvas in the Solent and also training her crew. As completed she had no bowsprit.*

they were speeding so fast that the Admiral's launch, which was secured to a battleship's boom as they sped by, was thrown up high by the wash. "We didn't wait to see what damage had been done but we raced on under the Fall River bridge and managed to lose the cutter. When we reached the boatyard we were quickly pulled out of the water as there was always someone waiting for this sort of emergency. If anyone had gone on board and felt our engines the heat would have given us away", he said.

I met Bill quite often in Looe in later days as he had made a hurried return to England after other similar incidents. I asked him recently if he would allow me to write about the day he called to me at Newport. He said, "Alfred, at one time I would not have dared for fear of being 'bumped off' but now prohibition is over I don't mind. I would never have dared rat on my mates who paid me plenty of bucks for running the speed boats. I might tell you that a New York newspaper offered me a large sum of money to give them the story of my experiences but if I had done it then I wouldn't be here now! I don't think I was doing anything very wrong because I was bringing in the best that money could buy, the real McCoy, not bootleg whiskey. I have seen bums in New York City draining out cocks in car radiators to get the alcohol which is used for preventing the systems from freezing. I hope some of the good stuff I brought in would have saved some of the drinkers from going blind on the bootleg stuff". So ends Bill's story, written in the same way in which he told it to me. While I was 'over there' I saw for myself quite a lot of intoxicating drink being bought and it seemed there was no problem to find it. The unfortunate aspect was the well offs were able to buy best quality British whiskeys while the poor were only able to afford the wood alcohol and even this wasn't cheap. We were told that many times blindness was caused by drinking this crude concoction. It was perhaps one of the most tragic and damaging items of legislation ever brought into operation in that great country.

Among many sightseeing trips perhaps the most interesting day we spent was at the Vanderbilt Estate where there was a complete Dutch village with people and animals living and working as near as possible to the way of life in Holland. At another part of the grounds there was housed a collection of English stage coaches, all polished as new and with their complete histories displayed. There were scores of silver plated harness for the many ponies in the stables nearby and also a large arena, completely covered over, where pony trotting races were held. Around the sides where the spectator accommodation was arranged there was a miniature rail track which was used to transport food and drink to the people watching the show. All these things amazed us and we had never seen anything on this scale before but now I'm afraid our round of social engagements had to finish for the time being.

On September 11th *Shamrock* was refloated and put out to moorings where she was prepared for a sail. We set out and bent the No. 3 mainsail but the wind quickly freshened and we were soon back at the buoy. The next day we sailed out with a reefed mainsail, jib and staysail and as we passed *H.M.S. Helliotrope* the crew gave us a hearty cheer. We returned at 3.30 p.m. and were now anxiously waiting for the next day and the first race of the contest.

At last it was here and the culmination of all these months of preparation. We left harbour under tow amidst much cheering from people ashore, blowing of hooters and sirens and accompanied by a host of craft of all shapes and sizes. The start was delayed from 11.50 a.m. to 1.00 p.m. because there was no wind. By then a light breeze had sprung up and its direction meant that the first leg of the contest was a dead run to the mark from the starting line. Both ships hoisted spinnakers but instead of running down wind, as we did, the American defender *Enterprise* went on a broad reach which gave her a faster point of sailing although it meant a longer distance to cover. This tactic paid off, however, for after going a certain distance she changed her spinnaker to the other side and went on a reach to the mark which despite sailing the longer course she reached two minutes ahead of *Shamrock*. Coming back to the starting and finishing line close hauled *Enterprise* beat us by 2½ minutes to win the race. The next day there was no racing and we spent the time giving the ship a good clean up, doing odd jobs and removing a ton of ballast.

On September 15th the race started at 11.50 a.m., on time, and consisted of a ten mile beat to windward then a ten mile reach and finally a ten mile run to the finishing line. Captain Heard put *Shamrock* in a splendid position at the start on the weather bow of *Enterprise* but despite this early advantage it was not long before we realised that the defender was sailing faster than we were. Even more important she was sailing nearer to the wind and she beat *Shamrock* to the first mark by 6 minutes increasing her lead to 9 minutes by the second mark. *Enterprise* finally led us home by 9½ minutes and all aboard our vessel were now beginning to realise that the odds were weighed heavily against us as I will explain later. Because of fog there was again no race the following day.

The next day, the eighteenth, the race got under way on time and began with a 15 mile beat to windward. Our Captain again took us across the line in a classic start with both ships on a starboard tack and *Enterprise* under our lee. After a few minutes the defender tacks and we follow but a short while after – disaster. As we go on another

The American defender Enterprise.

tack our main halyards capstan brake carried away and this put us out of the race. It would have made little difference to the outcome as *Enterprise* had already passed through our lee and come out and up on our weather bow. So back we went to harbour to refit.

The next day both yachts were on the line for a good start dead on 11.50 a.m. The first leg was 10 miles to windward and it was not long before *Enterprise* was well in the lead and she beat us to the first mark by 9½ minutes. A reach of 10 miles followed and we were able to pick up 2 minutes and improved on this on the final leg but were still 5 minutes behind *Enterprise* at the finish and thus ended the 1930 America's Cup races.

What were the odds against *Shamrock?* Perhaps the most important factor was that the Americans had built four ships, *Whirlwind, Yankee, Weatamoe* and *Enterprise.* These vessels raced together throughout the summer until just before the start of the Cup Races in September when the fastest of the four was chosen to be the defender. *Enterprise* and her 30 man crew were thus trained to perfection and in splendid racing trim whereas *Shamrock* and her 22 hands had been wearied by the crossing of the Atlantic and had not raced at all since the 6th July in Scotland.

The construction of the two vessels was also very different. *Shamrock* was built of three inch planking on steel frames, known as composite building. *Enterprise* was built of light sheet bronze about the thickness of an old penny piece. This allowed more space in the hull and thus more buoyancy. *Shamrock's* mast was of wood and estimated to be 1½ tons heavier than that of *Enterprise* which was fabricated in duralumin, a very light alloy. This difference in mast weights meant that *Shamrock* needed an extra 12 tons of lead in the keel. *Shamrock's* main boom was of orthodox shape, that is pear shaped in circumference with a track on the narrow, fore and aft, top to secure the foot of the mainsail. This meant that for several feet up and along the length of its foot the sail was absolutely flat, thus losing much of its power. *Enterprise* had what was known as a Park Avenue boom, shaped like a cigar cut through the middle with a series of tracks fitted across the boom at short intervals. The centre of the boom was four feet wide on top and on each track was a hank fastened to the foot rope of the sail. This allowed the bottom of the mainsail to slide to leeward four feet at the centre then at each track fore and aft of this a little less according to the track lengths so that at each end of the boom the foot of the sail was secured to the shortest track. This created a curve in the foot of the sail which gave it more power when close hauled.

All *Shamrock's* running gear, sheet tackles, falls for main runners and backstays, in fact all ropes and tackle for working the ship, were on deck and had to be manhandled. By comparison below deck *Enterprise* was full of winches to which all the above mentioned sheets, tackles, falls and the like were attached. Except steering, all the work of handling the ship when beating to windward was done below deck and this was a tremendous advantage in speed of handling. More than a third of *Enterprise's* crew were below all the time. In sailing, the helmsman gave directions to a mate who was stationed in a cockpit on the after side of the mast, which was open to below deck. The mate passed on the orders to the men working the winches, so with good co-ordination they were able to manoeuvre *Enterprise* very much faster than our crew were able to do. Comparing the two craft was like putting a Ford car against a new Rolls Royce!

The races were not won by any superior skill or seamanship but on the drawing board and with all the money the Americans were able to pour into the preparations. Camper and Nicholson, of Gosport, had built a first class racing yacht by British standards but it was a very long way behind American standards of racing craft at that time. It can be said that the actual racing was comparatively easy, out in the open sea with only two vessels as against competing with four or five other ships in the fairly restricted waters of the Solent. *Shamrock V* was now towed to Herreshoff's Boat Yard at Bristol, Rhode Island, to be prepared for the journey back.

After the Cup races our crew were able to relax and go ashore on leave as none had been allowed since two days before the first race. A farewell dinner was given to the two crews at the Hotel Belvedere, Bristol, on September 25th. The crew of the *Enterprise* were almost entirely Scandinavian, including the skipper and they were very friendly and excellent seamen. Many of them joined *Shamrock* so they could go home to Scandinavia for the winter after the summer season racing in American waters. Our contract had ended so all our crew took leave of Bristol and embarked on a large river boat — appropriately named *Plymouth* — for the journey to New York where we boarded the 34,000 ton Cunard liner *Caronia* for our passage home to Plymouth. My wife and very young son Terry were on the ship's tender in the Sound to meet me as were many wives and relations of our West Country members of *Shamrock's* crew. After all the farewells and best wishes had been said all round we split up and were on our separate ways to our respective towns. Thus ended an experience that will always remain in the memory of those who took part in it.

Shamrock V *racing in the Solent in 1931, in a fresh wind she is double reefed with small jib and staysail. Since her attempt to win the America's Cup she has been fitted with a short bowsprit.*

THE CHOIR AND BACK TO SHAMROCK.

For the drift net fishing the following winter I rejoined my father and his brother Ernest who was the engineer on *Our Daddy*. After each winter season it became the custom to hold a service of thanksgiving in the local chapel. This was known as The Harvest of the Sea, and the chapel was decorated with nets which had imitation fish in them, also crab pots, lamps, flags, lifebuoys and in fact anything used on a fishing boat. Very often the preacher was himself a fisherman but the service mainly consisted of singing of Sankey hymns all with a bearing on the sea. People would pack into the chapel and gained a lot of pleasure from taking part.

A choir had been formed from among the fishermen and their conductor was Harold Mutton, skipper of the fishing boat *Seagull*, who was a member of a very musical family in Looe. The choir gradually progressed into four part harmony and after learning many songs were soon in demand for concerts in the nearby towns. At Devonport, during the First World War, I had been a boy soprano in the St. Albans Choir for four years and this earlier training helped me when I became a baritone soloist in the fishermen's choir. One of the highlights in our singing career was a weekend in London. We gave a concert in the Central Hall, Westminster, at the invitation of the London Cornish Society Festival and we also paid a visit to the B.B.C. where we appeared on the "In Town Tonight" programme with the late Richard Dimbleby. We made many broadcasts and recordings but unfortunately these were lost in the blitz on London in the Second World War. We also had a week's engagement at the Palace Theatre, Plymouth, with two shows a night and we were invited to go on a road tour with one of the famous band leaders of the time. This, of course, was not possible as it would have meant some of the boats would have been laid up with no crews but it was a great temptation at a time when fishing was not very profitable.

All our services and concerts were given free in aid of many different charities with the exception of the B.B.C. performance and the week at the Palace. During our 26 years of singing we raised many thousands of pounds for worthy causes and gave pleasure to countless number of people. One pleasing aspect of all this was that whenever the Looe boats were working away from home at Plymouth, Brixham or Newlyn, it would not be long before the members of the choir would get together in a ship's cabin or the seamen's mission house and start singing lustily which they really enjoyed. Sometimes on the fish quays at night, after an evening out and before going back aboard to sleep, the men would be having their own vesper and very nice it would sound across the still waters. When fishing from Newlyn the crews often made their way home at weekends and hired a coach for the trip. It was certain we should be singing on the way and were usually booked to give a concert when we arrived to the delight of both the audiences and ourselves.

Having joined the Royal Naval Reserve earlier on it was our duty to go for two weeks training every two years. Having completed one such period serving on the 35,000 ton battleship *Rodney*, with three triple 16" gun turrets, fishermen like me felt completely out of place. The Admiralty then decided that fishermen should be trained in minesweeping on Government trawlers so my next period was served at Portland. With me, from Looe, was Dick Stephens and also my shipmate for many years on *Our Daddy*, Leonard Lamerton. We went to sea on trawlers to practice sweeping techniques and found this much more to our liking. While at Portland I passed an examination for leading seaman which in trawler language was bosun. Towards the end of the first week we had received no wages and our combined finances were getting rather strained. After an evening at the cinema we felt hungry and realising that there would be no food for us when we got back to base we stopped outside a restaurant and read the menu. After great deliberation we collected our odd coppers, boldly walked in and ordered a cup of tea and a sandwich each. Luckily the next day was pay day. Although we are not unpatriotic in any way it was not for reasons of patriotism that we had joined the R.N.R. but the fact was that a retaining fee of eight pounds per year was paid by the Government to claim our services at any time of crisis. This money could be drawn quarterly and was a great help towards the rent or rates for a married man.

In the spring of 1931 I was off to join the big yachts once again. Jack, Joe and I journeyed to the Southampton Yard of Camper & Nicholson to become part of the crew of *Shamrock V*. When the yacht was fitted out each man was handed certain items of clothing to wear for racing or going ashore. We received two jerseys with the name of the ship and the owners sailing club initials on the front, two pairs of trousers, white duck suits to be worn when racing, a peak cap, best shoes and plimsoles. These items became our property at the end of the season. Sir Thomas Lipton was a member of the Royal Ulster Yacht Club of Ireland and the emblem of the club was a "bloody hand". Legend has it that when the first boat carrying men to the coast of Ireland approached land one man was so anxious to be the first that he cut off his hand and threw it ashore. Before we commenced racing all our jerseys were called back to the yacht clothing outfitters because Sir Thomas had been made a member of the Royal Yacht Squadron. After all the many years of his racing service it was to be in his last that this honour was bestowed on him, almost too late for him to appreciate it. The initials R.U.Y.C. were removed from our jerseys and in their place were sewn the letters R.Y.S.

The fishermen's choir. Above: All ready for a Sunday night concert at the Cinema, Looe. Below: Conductor Harold Mutton says, "Try this one, boys" and holds an impromptu practice on the quayside.

We then began the tour of the season's regattas but one particular incident stands out in my memory. We were racing at Torbay in company with the other big yachts, including King George V's *Britannia,* in a stiff westerly wind. At the start of the race the wind was in an offshore direction and as soon as we crossed the line all ships hoisted their spinnakers on the starboard side with the mainsail eased out to port. The very large spinnaker, filled with wind, was sheeted out from the mast on a 60 ft. boom from the outer end of which a wire was led to the stern. There was another wire led forward to the bow so that the crew could control the sail both forward and aft on orders from the sailing master. As we raced across the bay to the first mark the wind veered more westerly and it was necessary to ease the boom forward. *Britannia* was so close on our port side, giving us a tight rope, that it became evident to our skipper as we neared the mark that it was going to be difficult to take down the spinnaker. Under these conditions it is the usual practice to alter course away from the wind for a few seconds in order to lower this huge sail easily. It was impossible to do this with *Britannia* luffing and forcing us more and more into the wind. Under the heavy strain the after wire suddenly parted and the boom jumped out of its socket on the mast. Up it went in the air and forward with the whole 3,700 square feet of silk sail — more than all the other sails put together. There was little we could do except pull out of the race and try and clear up the mess. Our second mate had a cut lip and one of the crew was knocked over the bow but fortunately he was able to grab the bowsprit shrouds and scramble back on board. The spinnaker wrapped round the topmast forestay tearing into shreds and, by the time we managed to get the boom back on deck and secured, the sail was a write off. When everything was shipshape we sailed back to Brixham where the second mate was taken ashore for stitches in his face. After all was made snug we had a meal, the first since the early morning.

The most important racing of the whole season's calendar was Cowes Week where would be gathered the largest concentration and assortment of craft. They ranged from 12 ft. dinghys to the huge 'J' class plus numerous pleasure boats, private yachts, cabin cruisers and always a naval vessel as guardship to *Britannia.* There was a fresh wind off the mainland across the Solent and this was making Cowes on a lee shore. Several other classes had started their races and the big yachts were under sail jockeying for position for the start of their contest. Ahead of us was *Britannia* on a starboard tack and she was well known to be a "dirty or wet" ship when racing in a breeze. This was because she was built with more fore and aft sheer than the newer ships which made her lower amidships and when heeling over in the wind she put her lee deck under water. It would need a very strong breeze to get this effect on *Shamrock V* which had been built with less pronounced sheer and was therefore higher in the centre.

We saw *Britannia* was well over with her deck under water amidships when suddenly we sensed there was something wrong aboard her. A member of the crew was waving his arms from the stern and she was gradually being brought up into the wind. One of the men on our foredeck shouted, "Captain, there's a man in the water". As we made for the spot we could see something in the water which looked like a person's head and we were prepared to go in after him as soon as we were close enough. Unfortunately in less than 100 yards we lost sight of him and he was not seen again until nine days later when the body was recovered off Ryde, farther down the coast. The dead man was Erny Friend of Brixham who, we were told later, was down on deck endeavouring to clear the main runner falls. This is a dead tackle used for tightening or loosening the main wire stays which are each side of the masthead and which run down to deck tackles on either side of the ship. As the vessel changes tack or alters course bringing the wind on the other beam it is necessary to taughten the masthead stay on the weather side to take the strain. All this had to be done in a few seconds as the ship swung round. As *Britannia* heeled over the rush of water along her deck swept Erny off his feet and dragged him along until he was forced to lose his grip from exhaustion and was swept overboard towards the stern. He was a fine man, respected by all who knew him and being the second mate had the responsibility of his ship and the well being of her crew always uppermost in his mind. The tragedy was made worse as Erny had a brother aboard with him who was taking part in his first yachting season. It was a sad day for us all in the 'J' class and their race was cancelled with flags flown at half mast by all the craft in the area and from Cowes.

Among the big yachts one ship I would like to mention was the schooner *Westward.* This large and beautiful American built vessel was the pride of the fleet and when racing in the Solent with a beam wind she could soar through the rest. She carried a large light main topmast staysail on these occasions which was christened the 'baby elephant'. She was owned by Mr. T. B. Davies who we referred to as the 'reverend gentleman' because he could be heard shouting at his crew in what might loosely be called a 'seaman like manner'. There always seemed to be a shortage of crew to handle this big ship and many times during the season naval ratings would sail as extra hands. *Westward* was a lovely sight under full sail and it was very sad to hear that when her owner died she was taken out to sea and scuttled which also became the fate of *Britannia* later when King George died. At the end of the summer *Shamrock V* was again laid up at Camper & Nicholson's Southampton yard and her gear stored, while we went home to the winter fishing.

His Majesty King George V's yacht Britannia *heeling over and this shows clearly her lee deck awash as mentioned in the text.*

The magnificent racing schooner Westward *with mast head man aloft.*

It was good to be back as there were few times during the whole six months of the yachting season that those of us from the Westcountry were able to spend even a day at home. We were better able to face up to the winters now as having worked on the yachts entitled us to employment cards on which we had affixed stamps all the summer. With the racing money we had received during the season plus the unemployment benefit we were able to draw when not fishing our financial position had improved considerably.

During the winter Sir Thomas Lipton died and *Shamrock V* was bought by Mr. Tom Sopwith of the aircraft firm. He had been very successful in the 12 metre class and his last one *Mouet,* a very fast boat, had been sold to an American after which no doubt, she helped to boost her class on that side of the Atlantic. Mr. Sopwith's skipper was Captain George Williams from Hamble and during the winter he wrote me asking if I would rejoin the crew of *Shamrock V* for the coming season. I replied I was pleased to accept. Unfortunately because of the hard work and irregular meals on the big yachts I had developed a serious stomach complaint and in February 1932 I underwent an operation which I hoped would put the matter right for the future. Six weeks later I was back on *Shamrock* and found my shipmates included many of the previous crew.

At this time there was acute depression throughout the country with a tremendous amount of unemployment in all classes of industry. Everyone was caught up in this one way or another and our crew were asked to take a cut in wages of about 10% which we had to reluctantly accept. I was again asked to run the ship's motor launch but instead of the normal 5/- extra per week I was only offered 2/6d. I had no hesitation in telling Captain Williams that I was not prepared to work all the extra hours of duty entailed in maintaining and running the launch very often when the rest of the crew were off duty. In the end the Captain saw my point and I was granted the five shillings as before.

We got on very well with the Captain and also his brother who was one of the crew. In one of the races during Cowes Week our ship won the 100 guineas Gold Cup and the owner, Mr. Sopwith, sent on board that evening six bottles of champagne for the crew. Captain George said to me, "Come on Alfred, have some of this stuff, it will be good for your stomach". I have never been used to strong drink but hoping his advice was good I emptied a tumbler and a half into my empty stomach. It was however my head which felt the effect and in a short while I began to sing much to the amusement of the lads in the forecastle and producing a wide grin from the Captain.

When we were racing Mr. Sopwith did most of the steering while his wife acted as timekeeper for crossing the line at the start. We considered they both did a good job. I never remember, however, that the owner at any time spoke to a crew member on board and it seemed very much a case of 'upstairs and downstairs' with the Captain in between. We had to accept this attitude of course as we were only paid hands working for someone else's pleasure.

The racing season proceeded with the big yachts going the rounds of the various ports and regattas but it was not very enjoyable for me as I had not recovered my health. Towards the end of the racing calendar, while at Plymouth, I had to leave the ship and enter hospital and thus ended my racing career. In October 1933 I received a letter from Captain Williams inviting me to join him on a new yacht called *Endeavour* which Mr. Sopwith was having built to challenge for the America's Cup in the following year. Unfortunately I had to refuse as I had been suffering from a perforated duodenal ulcer and this meant a strict diet for many years to come. I had therefore to say a final goodbye to the big yachts and make the best of it at home for a living.

In 1974 Shamrock *was discovered in Italian hands and with a new name. She was brought back to Camper & Nicholsons and refitted but not with her original rig or lofty mast.*

NEW RESPONSIBILITIES, THEN WAR.

My wife and I saved a little money so we decided the best thing for me was to have a little boat of my own and do some crabbing etc. I ordered a 24 footer from boatbuilders Frank Curtis & Larney Mitchell at a cost of £64 and I bought a secondhand engine for £24. We made a number of crab pots with the intention of my completing the winter fishing with my father on *Our Daddy* and then, in the spring, to fit out and work my own boat which I was quite looking forward to. It was not to be for in late December my father was taken ill while fishing out of Plymouth and had to be rushed home. He passed away within the week on Boxing Day, a tragic blow to all the family.

My grandfather still owned *Our Daddy* and he asked me to take my father's place as skipper which, after much heart searching, I agreed to do. It was not an easy decision to make at the age of 27 taking charge of a lugger with a crew of men much older than myself and with the personal emotional strain involved. All my plans and thoughts of branching out on my own had to be put aside and I sold my little boat before she was launched. After our sad Christmas I took skipper of *Our Daddy* and we fished throughout the winter with the other Looe boats. We were long lining in the spring and then after July we prepared for the pilchard season at Newlyn.

During 1934 I joined the St. John's Ambulance Division. My main reason for this was that being a seaman in the R.N.R. it was possible that at some future date when under training I could sit for a mates ticket in the trawlers and for that it was necessary to hold a first aid certificate. When several of us had obtained these we formed a Looe Division with our local doctor as Divisional Surgeon and, having purchased a two-wheeled stretcher we undertook voluntary duty in the town. A few years later we acquired a new ambulance and built our own garage and headquarters at the Millpool, West Looe. We were given a great deal of financial support from the townsfolk and we got a lot of pleasure in helping less fortunate people. I also became a founder member of the Looe branch of the Toc H movement so beside trying to earn a living at sea I had plenty of social work to keep me busy ashore.

The winter fishing of 1934 was no better than the previous ones and during the latter end of the year some of our boats went up to Brixham to try for herring. The fishing area was further up the coast off Budleigh Salterton and Beer and the herring were of smaller size than we had been used to catching in our home waters. Late one evening we left Looe to steam for nine hours to reach the fishing grounds. On arrival we spotted a white light low in the water and when we approached we saw three men in a boat hoisting their drift net full of herring by a tackle on the mast. I hailed them and asked what things were like and back came the reply, "Is that you Alfred?" The skipper was Captain Sanders of Brixham with his two sons Fred and Harry and he had recognised my voice at once. He had been our Torbay pilot firstly on *Astra* and later on *Shamrock V* while his two sons had been on *Astra* as extra hands while racing in the area. He told us to go straight to windward of his boat about the length of our nets and then shoot towards him. This we promptly did and then settled the watch with one man as lookout while the rest of the crew got in some sleep. One never really knew when the herring would swim in and get enmeshed but all remained quiet until daylight. In the early morning the seagulls began to hover over sensing that the fish were moving in the nets. The wonderful instinct of these birds is amazing at times like this. We pulled on board a good catch of some 20 cran of herring and another boat from Looe, *Our Boys,* which had joined us also had a good haul. We made £60 at the fish market sale and were very pleased with our night's work.

The weather settled in bad for the following few days and when we returned to the grounds there were no herring to be found. We had however, brought with us an escallop dredge that my father had made some years before at Brixham and we now tried this out in company with other boats from Exmouth and Brixham. Our dredge was a large one of nine feet across the mouth which enabled us to keep up with the top boats catchwise, although the first time we tried it we shot it over the side upside down and drew a blank! After a short season with the dredge we left for home to dry our drift nets and prepare for long lining.

Generally there was no living to be had at all the year fishing. The young men were able to crew on the yachts during the summer to augment their wages but I was no longer able to do this. I laid up *Our Daddy* in the middle of the year and took a job handling a small motor launch for a local boatman running trips to Polperro, Fowey, Mevagissey and taking fishing parties out in the bay. My wages were only £2 per week although I did receive a few tips. All in all it was not a great amount and I am sure my wife had the hardest time keeping our family fed and clothed particularly as we had two sons by this time, Terry and David, with a little more than two years between their ages. Let no one say these were the good old days although no doubt they differed according to one's circumstances. During the whole of the 1936 winter fishing, from November 12th to January 23rd, each member of the crew of our boat only received as his share, £19. 15s. The boat was of course laid up during the summer months. During the 1937 winter the crews' share was £23.19s per man for the period November 13th to January 8th. This was derived from a mixed bag of pilchards, herring and mackerel.

Nearing the end of a day's fishing with the net room overflowing and boxes of fish on deck. The mackerel wheels are seen fitted on the bulwarks and the white gut used is 250 lb. breaking strain. The gut trace being held in the hands of Terry Pengelly (my son) is 120 lb. breaking strain.

Colin Matthews heaving in the long line with squirming mackerel attached.

In 1939 the pattern of life changed dramatically. In the spring my grandfather died and he left *Our Daddy* between my uncle and myself but I am afraid at the time it was more of a liability than an asset. Once again during the summer she was laid up and I ran a cabin cruiser for the same firm as before but with my wages increased to the princely sum of £2.10s. per week. Then in September war was declared and as a Royal Naval Reservist I was at once called up. With several other Looe men I went to Lowestoft which was then the main base for Naval trawlers. This was our second trip to Lowestoft in 12 months but this time it was more serious. On our arrival we reported to the R.N.R. Headquarters which was in a theatre at Sparrow's Nest and we were then billeted out in boarding houses with orders to report back in the morning. Before being drafted as crew members to the trawlers we had to undergo a medical examination by Naval doctors, but this I failed to pass as I was under strict diet treatment from my doctor. After a few days at Lowestoft I was handed a medical discharge and with three other men sent home as unfit to serve in the trawlers.

Shortly after arriving back home we fitted out for the winter season and of course while I was on my own boat I was able to eat the special diet I needed for my condition. By this time I had risen to an Ambulance Officer in St. John's and with the country at war this became more important and demanding. Many families and large numbers of children were evacuated from the London area down to our part of the country. These required extra facilities including a maternity home which was set up in a large private house named Polvellan. We had recruited several volunteer drivers for the ambulance who were willing to be called on day or night and we worked out a rota system to spread the hours. Many times I had to leave my bed for ambulance duty after having been at sea for several nights. The complicated maternity cases always seem to happen at night which meant a trip to Redruth, some fifty miles, so we were kept busy one way or another.

Through the winter of 1939 we worked off the coast at night with the drift nets and strange as it may seem there were much more fish to be caught. In the following spring we were long lining and all the boats kept close together as with France overrun and E-boats active in the channel it became increasingly dangerous to venture far. Sometimes we fished up to 28 miles south south west of the Eddystone and frequently we were visited by our Naval patrols to see that all was well. We were finally ordered to fish inside the three mile limit and our last long line trips were close inshore off Salcombe for ray and conger.

One morning early we were called out of bed by the Naval Department. At the time our troops were being brought back from the French beaches and all available boats were ordered to Plymouth to assist in the evacuation. We hurriedly unloaded all our fishing gear on to the quay and then steamed our boats to Plymouth where we took on oil and provisions in preparation for the crossing. There is of course a great difference in the distance from Plymouth to France compared with that from Dover. It is approximately 100 mile across the Channel here and we were wondering how our engines, some rather ancient, would stand up to the long trip. We laid in Sutton Harbour for two days at one hour's notice and all hands had to remain aboard. We were then told that the larger ships of the evacuation fleet were able to take off the troops and so our trip was cancelled and we were sent back home. One very unfortunate incident during the operation was the sinking of the ex-liner *Lancastria,* of 16,000 tons, with troops on board and a great many were lost. I was on ambulance duty the next day visiting a Plymouth hospital when some of the survivors were brought in for treatment and it was a very sad sight.

In July 1940 we were stopped from fishing altogether as there was fear of an invasion. Our town was ringed with barbed wire on the seaward side with tank traps everywhere and gun emplacements all along the sea front at Hannafore. The Nazilee Hotel became the headquarters for the troops stationed in Looe, while wire boom defences were laid across the harbour mouth and all lighting blacked out at night. Many of us went to work at the boatyard where they were building large motor launches (M.L.s) for the Navy. The greater part of East Looe quay was taken over and sheds were built for storing equipment for the craft being built. Large wooden minesweepers were also brought to Looe to be fitted out with engines and other gear.

Working on shore gave me more time for ambulance duty and as several of our St. John's men were working at the same boatyard we were allowed to leave the job at anytime for emergency work. We also joined the Civil Defence with our headquarters at the Tregertha Hotel and there was another first aid post at West Looe. As trained ambulance personnel we took on the job of instructing the home guard members in first aid. I remained working at the boatyard until late in the winter of 1941 when the fishing restrictions were lifted a little and smaller boats were allowed to work close inshore.

I took charge of a 24 ft. craft named *Margarite*, owned by Jack Soady, and I worked on my own for a few months fishing for conger and whiting. One morning when not far from Looe Island I baited and shot a small box of long line and to my surprise I caught 33 turbot. This was a good catch and it was not long before the other boats were trying for this fish. During May 1941 further restrictions were lifted so we fitted out *Our Daddy* with drift nets for pilchard fishing. This had to be done at night and we had to haul in our nets blind as complete darkness had to be maintained on deck and only a small shaded lamp permitted below. It was dangerous to even strike a match for fear of attracting an enemy craft of some sort. It was surprising how we got used to handling the nets in the dark and picking out the fish but we did welcome moonlight nights when working under these conditons.

There was one very noticeable change during the first two years of the war and this was that for the first time in twenty years we were able to fish for pilchards off Looe in the summer months. Previously this had only been possible off Mounts Bay and obviously the movement of fish had changed to bring the shoals further up the coast. It is true to say that with the Navy taking over many craft for minesweeping and coastal patrol work there had been a big drop in commercial fishing and of course the French and Belgian trawler fleets were not operating in our waters. There was certainly a marked increase in the fish stocks during this period.

When the ban on night fishing was lifted a regulation was brought in that boats leaving harbour at night were handed by the local Naval Officer a letter of the alphabet in the morse code enclosed in a sealed envelope to be opened at sea. Each port had its own distinguishing letters and every night a different one was used. On returning, during the hours of darkness, we were challenged by the service lookout with a flashing torch and we had to reply in morse with the night's code letter and if all was well and the tide right we were allowed to enter harbour.

One winter's night the fishing had been light and the fleet had become spread out while searching for shoals by brimming as described earlier. With no lights allowed on deck and no means of communication between the boats we were very much on our own at sea during the night. It was fine and we had been searching for more than an hour with one of the crew up in the bows thumping a heavy weight on the deck at intervals trying to disturb any fish which might be lazing underneath. Suddenly we came upon a large shoal which began to swim away as we passed through and the silver reflection of this mass moving through the phosphorescence lit up our boat. We promptly manoeuvered the ship into a position to shoot the nets and when this was completed we stopped engines and lay quietly moored up to the net. It was then time for tea and a snack.

As we lay there in the quiet of the night we could hear fish leaping out of the water all round the boat which was a good sign that we had shot at least some of the nets through the shoal. After one hour had passed it was time to have a 'look up', that is pull up the end of the net to see if any fish were enmeshed and sure enough there were plenty to be seen. After another hour it was decided to haul in the catch and get back to harbour, to catch the tide. Because of the deep draft our boat could only enter up to three hours on either side of high water, that means on flood or ebb tide. There were very many more fish in the nets by now so to save time we just pulled them on board and straight down into the net room with the fish enmeshed. When it was full below we piled the rest on deck where it looked like a silver pyramid. We had done very well so we started up engines and made a run for home.

It is not easy to find you way at night without any lights ashore even on a coast you know and the wind freshened as we rounded Looe Island which slowed up us. We found we had missed the tide by an hour and this meant we should have to lay up in some sheltered quarter for the next five hours. We dropped anchor in the lee of the Island and all on board went below except for one man. This was a friend of mine, Harold Cox, who worked for the gas company and had come out that night for the trip. All was quiet and the crew tucked in to their meal with a mug of tea being passed up to Harold on deck. Suddenly all hell broke loose. Harold shouted down the hatch, "They are firing at us from the shore". There was no need to tell us, as tracer bullets were flying over the mast like shooting stars and rapid machine gun fire was coming from one of the sites at Hannafore, controlled by the Army. As we scrambled up on deck we were blinded by a searchlight and it was impossible for us to make them see the night's identification signal from our torch. We held up our nets with the fish in to show them who we were but in any case we were so close in that our registration number painted on the bows should have been clearly recognisable.

A few minutes later the scare died down and a small motor boat approached us flashing a light, to which I replied with the signal for the night. It was manned by Harry Hocking and Maurice Pengelly who were employed by the Navy and they came alongside. They soon understood what had happened and were able to report back to the officer in charge. We spent the rest of the night cleaning out our nets which in the dark was a work of art. After we had returned to harbour in the morning and landed our catch an Army officer came down to the boat and requested that I go with him. At the Army headquarters the Battery Commander ordered me to hand over my fishing permit without waiting for me to explain and this meant that my boat could not leave the harbour until it was returned to me. He told me that had I attempted to move away from the Island he had ordered the heavy guns to be trained on me and I would have been treated as an enemy vessel and blown out of the water. I thanked him for those kind words and left. I had already been told by the local policeman, earlier that morning, that he had recognised our boat in the searchlight beam and had informed the Battery Commander who we were and what we were doing there but the latter being 'not quite himself' at the time took no notice of the information.

The next thing I was told that two days hence I was to report to the Naval Commander at Fowey who was in charge of all craft in the area. I had always felt more at ease with the Navy being able to speak the same language of the sea as it were but his first words, however, startled me. He said, "I understand you have been giving a lot of trouble at Looe over a period". Knowing that it was in this officer's hands whether or not we should be able to continue fishing I replied, "Sir, I am prepared to go to court with my crew to refute that allegation. We have given no trouble and in fact the incident was not my fault as we were not challenged when we entered the bay at Looe". He then asked, "Why cannot all your boats go to sea and come back together?" Having explained at length the reasons why this was impossible when night fishing, I felt that he was believing me and understanding the situation. Very soon our conversation became normal and matter of fact as it should be between two seafaring men. Finally he shook hands with me, wished me luck and what was more important he gave me back my fishing permit. Not very long after, by a coincidence the Battery Commander was given another post away from Looe!

Despite this incident there was more danger from being spotted by enemy aircraft and this did sometimes happen with boats being fired on. Many nights during the heavy bombing of Plymouth, the German planes would fly over us on the way in and then turn over the land to drop their bombs on the way out to sea. On some of the nights it looked as though everything was ablaze and the sky was filled with a great glow of fire which made us wonder if anything could possibly be left by the next morning. From the sea it was a sight we shall never forget. Sometimes an aircraft dropped its bombs in the water and the shock of the explosion would hit our propellor shaft as if someone was striking it with a hammer.

There were times when having been at sea all night and witnessed a heavy raid on Plymouth it was my turn of duty the following morning to take a patient by ambulance to a hospital in the City. With so much devastation it was often impossible to find a way through the streets and we had to be directed by another route. One morning we were called upon to use our ambulance to help evacuate a ward that had been damaged and there was also fear of an unexploded bomb nearby. One had to witness the wonderful devotion to duty of the nursing staff and the very cool and efficient way in which they did their job in an emergency. It was an inspiration to us all and was for certain a tremendous help to the patients at a time like this. One great thing stood out amidst all the danger, fears and suffering and that was the wonderful spirit of cooperation and friendliness shown by all concerned in welfare work of any kind.

Our Daddy *leaving Looe and on the cliffs above are hotels on the Hannafore road.*

HELPING TO FILL THE NATION'S LARDER.

We now fitted out *Our Daddy* with trawling gear that had lain idle in the store for twenty years. During the following winter's drift net fishing increasing amounts of palagic fish were caught with our largest haul of all time being on the 29th November 1941. It was a very fine evening and while in company with several other boats we noticed birds working busily over what we thought must be a shoal. The sea was oily, gannets were diving and all nature's signs were there to see. We shot our nets in a straight line before the wind and when the job was completed the boat was brought round head to wind with a rope from the end of the nets attached to a cleat on the bow. The mizzen sail was hoisted aft and sheeted tightly in the middle and this would keep us lying with the bow pointing directly into the wind ready to haul in the nets when ready. All hands then went to tea and we waited until dark when we hoped the fish would swim into the nets. We had not long to wait.

As the daylight was fading we heard the screeching of gulls over the nearest boat and in the dimming light we could see the men pulling in their nets, full of fish. Hastily gulping down our tea we donned oilskins and sea boots and went forward to see if we too were lucky. When we pulled up the end of our net there was not a fish to be seen so we dropped it back into the water and stopped on deck having a yarn. After a few minutes my uncle looked out forward in the direction of the floats attached to the top of the nets. These are fastened every few fathom by a strop some 18 ft. long thus hanging the nets below the surface. "Do you see any of the buoys (floats)", he said. In answer to his question we all looked out ahead but there was nothing to be seen except oily water. A very heavy concentration of fish had swum into the nets and the force of their movement plus their combined weight had pulled nets and floats below the surface. We rushed to prepare for hauling in and by fixing a long roller on the starboard rail of the bulwarks we were able to spread the net and pull it in like a large blanket.

We were a four man crew with two standing below in the net room to store it as it came down and one man up forward pulling in the head rope or top of the net with the other man standing aft heaving in the bottom or skirt of the net. The boat was moving gently forward on her engine and with a slight swell she was rolling a bit. When she went to port all hands hung on to the net then when she rolled to starboard it was possible to haul a length on board and down into the large room below deck. It was so full of pilchards, mackerel and herring that it was almost impossible to see the mesh, it was just one mass of silver fish. There was so much that it took us several hours to get it all aboard and then much of the catch remained on deck piled up like a hayrick. At one time while we were hauling in we heard a noise like an aeroplane engine which startled us. The moon was shining and looking over the sea we suddenly realised that the noise was caused by a mass of fish that had risen to the surface and were leaping out of the water in millions all around us.

Eventually we made for home and standing in the wheelhouse I could just look over the top of the piled up net and fish to see where to steer. We were loaded down in the water like a London barge. When we arrived in harbour there were many people on the quay to see the boats come in and I engaged 5 men to help us shake out the fish so we were nine clearing the nets. Spars were rigged across the boat and the net was taken forward over them with men working on both sides to clear the fish. When a length had been cleared it was pulled forward and stowed in the bows while another section was heaved on to the spars. The decks were soon full of fish and it was then packed into baskets and taken on to the quay to be placed in barrels ready for the fish buyers to see the next morning. The operation went on through the night and all next day until dark when the deck was cleared but there was still some that had dropped through below into the fish room. We sprinkled this with salt and left it until the next morning.

All through the work our womenfolk had been bringing sandwiches and tea or cocoa to us at frequent intervals so that we did not have to break off for a meal. We had caught 2,000 stone of fish that night but it was very hard work and the pulling on the nets had made our hands sore and blistered. With such a heavy catch we were lucky indeed to have saved our nets and we were thankful to see the end of it and have a good night's sleep.

The fish stocks in the channel had obviously improved and here are figures to prove this. During the winter months from October to December 1942 the 23 boats — of different sizes — working out of Looe had landed 45,159 stone of pilchards. In the same period of 1943 this had risen to 109,249 stone and all of this was distributed as fresh fish in this country, a great help when so much of our food had to be brought in by sea in the teeth of the U-boats. One day I remember sixty tons of fish leaving Looe by rail to help the nation's larder, most of it destined for the Welsh mining areas. As far as I know during the war years was the only time that Cornish pilchards were being delivered around this country to be eaten fresh from the sea.

The pattern of our fishing during 1941, 1942 and 1943 was drifting for pilchards in the spring and early summer then fitting out for trawling which carried on until November. The boats would go over to drift net fishing until January. On August 28th 1943 my wife presented me with a daughter who we named Julie. This event took place twelve years after our second son David was born and now our family was complete.

One day in 1944, while we were at sea trawling, we saw a large concentration of ships steaming up the channel towards us from the west. There were all kinds of vessels many flying balloons and including several large landing craft. It was common knowledge that there were fleets of ships in our Westcountry ports and that Cornwall was full of American troops. Many of our roads and byways were jammed full of vehicles of all descriptions for weeks on end. It was a heartening sight to witness this tremendous movement of men and materials and it took no stretch of imagination to realise what was taking place. We were in the midst of the fleet for the American sector of the invasion of France. The following morning on the radio confirmed that it was D day and all that it entailed in the landing of masses of troops and equipment. There is no doubt that it was a wonderfully planned operation.

During the summer of 1944, we commenced long lining again, working gear with the hooks much closer together spaced 4 ft. apart instead of the usual eight to nine feet apart on the main line. This enabled us to use less length of long line with the usual number of hooks. There was very good fishing to be had nearer home, approximately 17 miles from the Eddystone, S.W. to S.E. There was no need to go out any further at this time, so all these things combined meant less time at sea and so lessened the danger from enemy craft on sea and in the air.

I had become busy at this time with added responsibility on shore. Unfortunately our Looe Ambulance Superintendent, Arthur Singleton, died under very tragic circumstances. I was asked to take his place, and this I accepted with misgivings as, being the skipper of a fishing vessel, much of my time was taken up in being at sea to secure a living for myself and crew. I wondered how long it would be possible for me to carry out the responsibility of being in charge of the ambulance work and carry it on in a proper manner. It meant taking all the ambulance calls by telephone, arranging for crews. If it happened that I was at sea, my wife had to get in touch with drivers and crew. I had to arrange for petrol that could only be had by coupon issued each month. After a while however, more telephones were installed by our Division into the homes of crew members and drivers. We were then able to draw up and work a rota system of duty. We had some thirty men and women St. John members and with our volunteer drivers, it became much easier for transport work. Everyone knew their hours of duty, only in an emergency did one have to call the nearest member at hand.

I was very fortunate in having a good crew in the boat. For the greater part of the war years I had a young Belgian fisherman with me, Jerome Daems, who had learnt his fishing in trawlers. He was a great help when we decided to do the trawl fishing although he had done no drifting or long lining before coming with me, but he very soon got used to it. When France and Belgium were overrun in the early part of the war many fishing families from these countries left their homes at short notice, leaving almost everything behind, and came across the Channel in their fishing boats to our West country ports. Some made their homes in Looe, several used their own boats with crews to fish from our port, others joined our local boats as crew members and were very friendly and excellent fishermen. They all settled into our community very well indeed, so well, that one or two married local girls and Belgian girls married our young men.

Towards the end of July 1945, some of our fishermen who had been away on war service were being sent home. My good friend and crew member, Leonard Lamerton, joined me once again and took charge of the engines on board. Another pal of mine, Jack Sargent, joined me in October and in the following June, Harold Tamblyn, came with us. We had all been together on the *Our Daddy* for many years before the war. Sad to relate, many of my pals and fishermen who had been with me through the years before, did not come back and it is only the relations and friends of those who have passed on who can remember with sadness and affection, those of our kind who gave their lives that we may carry on to the end.

A. J. Pengelly in the uniform of Superintendent of the Looe Division of St. John's Ambulance Brigade.

Alfred John Pengelly surveys a mass of fish on the foredeck of Our Daddy *and is preparing to load and weigh it in boxes on the quayside.*

Frank Pengelly and his crew hauling in nets at night.

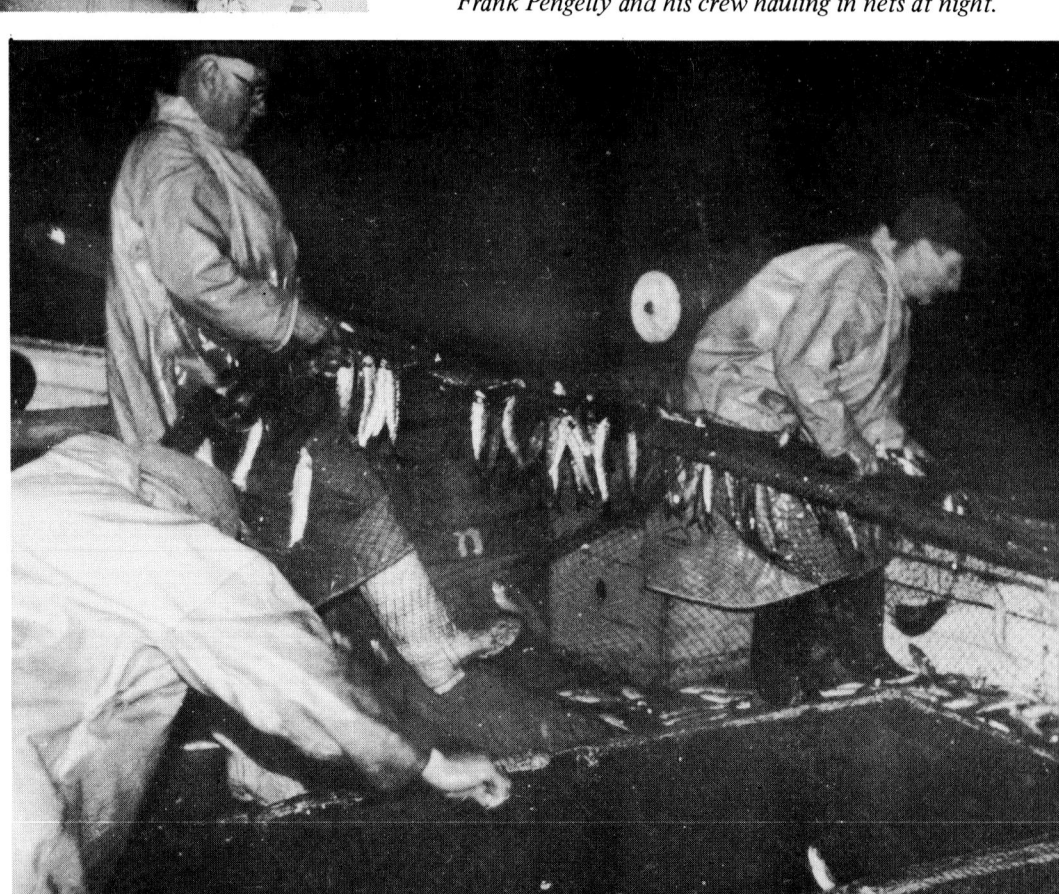

POST WAR TROUBLES AND TRIALS.

The fishing had improved considerably by the end of the war years and during November and December 1945, one of our local pilchard curers had salted down into concrete tanks 150 tons of pilchards. After curing these fish were packed into barrels and distributed abroad by the United Nations food organisation.

The demand for Cornish pilchards changed considerably after the war. Because of the increased landings of white fish into our larger ports, pilchards became unacceptable on the fresh fish markets of our country, plus the fact that the demand for salt cured pilchards to Italy had now become very limited as the eating habits of the Italian people had changed over the war years. It became important to our Industry that a new outlet be found.

After the winter fishing, we fitted out long lining and carried on until the following winter season. It became necessary after a few seasons to alter our gear somewhat, by extending the length of line and securing the hooks and strops further apart on the line as in pre war days, with the long line approximately seven miles in length with more than six thousand hooks attached. We had to fish further from home as the nearer grounds were fished out and with the fish stock being depleted, the long line had to cover more of the sea bed. Our first long line trip after the war to the deeper fishing grounds was on the 28th March 1948. Much of the gear was brand new and in the company of two other Looe luggers, *Our Boys* and *Our Girls*, we steamed 45 miles S.E. by S. from the Eddystone. This took us more than eight hours from home steaming time. In the morning, as daylight was coming in, we shot our lines with the flood or east going tide. When all the line was laid we then remained alongside of the marker dhan waiting for the tide to turn to ebb, also for all hands to have a fry-up for breakfast.

To the eastward we saw approaching five craft which, when coming nearer, proved to be trawlers from Caen in France. They were trawling with their fishing gear on the bottom and heading directly for our long line laid on the bottom also. We endeavoured to keep them clear of our gear laid in their path, but it was no use as the French fishermen refused to alter course. The boat, *Our Girls,* went alongside theirs and asked them to steer away from our gear but they took no notice, crossing with heavy equipment cutting our fishing lines to pieces. We did not know at that time that there was a considerable amount of fish in that area. When we commenced hauling our long line, we realised what the fishing was like. In the end we were only able to retrieve one third of the line we had shot, the remainder of the gear had been cut and swept away by those Frenchmen.

In broad daylight, it was a very deliberate attack on our fishing gear. We saved parts of our long line where the marker dhans were attached to it. Our catch was entirely of thorne back rays, 480 stone — a record catch for us on approximately one third of the gear. The other Looe boats with us were treated the same as we were and lost part of their fishing gear. Getting back to port we reported the incident, there was a Ministry investigation and a fishing vessel was sent to Caen to make enquiries. We got little redress however, as we had lost a good catch of fish and had to remain in harbour for two weeks, working to replace the lost gear. Finally we received part payment from our own Government.

Throughout the long line seasons for many years we have been pestered by these French trawlers in the Channel. I always consider that Nelson should have done a better, perhaps more complete, job.

The marketing of pilchards began to improve because of a steady and increasing demand from one or two canning factories that had been built and were in operation already for other kinds of food processing and now commenced to can pilchards. Within two years demand had been built up to supply five canning factories both winter and summer and this extended the pilchard fishing to approximately nine months of the year. Most of the fish prices had been under a control laid down by the Government since early in the war and these were carried on for a few years after. In fact with the increasing cost of fishing equipment and the general rise in the cost of living, fishermen were forced to ask that the fish sales be taken off control, also to ask for a subsidy of so much per stone of fish to help in the running expenses of the vessel. At the time pilchard, mackerel and herring were controlled at 3/6d. per stone, ray and skate at 4/6d. per stone, whale meat however, was controlled at 5/6d. per stone.

In the summer the Cornish fleet of drifters were based at Newlyn for the pilchard fishery. One day in late afternoon the boats left harbour to work four to five miles south east of the Wolf Rock lighthouse. Arriving on the fishing grounds there were little signs of fish, as is often the case during the summer. The boats began to shoot their nets well clear of one another and it was a gamble as to who would have the best catch. During the first part of the operation the wind was light North westerly and we were running gently before it. By the time the last nets were shot the light was beginning to fade. The crew then cleared the decks in preparation for hauling in the nets later and mast head and riding lights were lit. At the windward end of the nets a dhan had been attached with a light on so that if, in case of trouble, it was necessary to move the boat to the other end of the gear we were able to see it and make for it. The boats were scattered over a wide area, almost as far as the eye could see and, with all the lights lit, it looked like a floating town.

Away to the west in the distance there seemed to be two lights, one under the other, and higher than the rest of the fleet. Taking little notice our crew went to supper, but it was always the custom for one crew member to keep watch on deck or at least pop up every few minutes to see that all was well. After a short time he reported that the two lights sighted earlier to the west were now closer and higher and beneath them were rows of other lights. It was a big ship coming in from the Atlantic and steaming through the fleet. We hastily finished our meal and put on our sea boots and oilskins in readiness for hauling in the nets. Other fishing boats in the path of the ship were showing flares made of oil soaked rags fastened to a metal handle in an attempt to attract her attention and cause her to alter course, away from our nets. She was coming closer to us and we were also showing a flare, but it was no use. As she came nearer, the two mast head lights were looking a little apart, which meant that she was not coming directly at us. The light on the foremast is always lower than the light on the after mast and by this time we could also see her green starboard light. We knew, however, that unless she altered course our nets would be severely damaged. This huge ship, lit up like a city in the dark, seemed to have little regard for us as she steamed through the fleet of boats. Although miraculously not hitting one, there was little we could do except to commence hauling our nets. As we were taking them on board, this ocean liner was passing at speed over our gear a few hundred yards ahead of the boat, many passengers lining the guard rails on deck looking down at us in our puny little boats. They were in evening dress, no doubt having a breather after their meal, and finding it great fun to see us so close, dressed up in our yellow oilskins, jumpers or smocks. If the Captain's ears were not buring at the time he must have been a very insensitive person. We hauled a length further, then came the damage. This very large deep draft vessel had cut our nets completely down through, her large propellors had played havoc with the very fine cotton nets, some of which could not be repaired or used anymore. Arriving in harbour the following morning, several skippers like myself were making for the Ministry of Agriculture and Fisheries Office at Newlyn to report the incident and the damage incurred, and Mr. Jeffery Wooleston, the Fishery Officer, had a busy day collecting details of the incident. The ship was the *Stattendam* of the Holland-American line coming home from America. However, after a long time the Company paid out compensation for all the damaged gear, but this did not pay us for all the time and effort in getting our fleet of nets back to normal. It is true, of course, that off the Mounts Bay area is a very busy place for shipping and using fleets of drift nets there is a hazard at best.

There was one very important thing that happened because of the controls imposed on fish sales. All fish had to be weighed at first hand sale and this was one of the best things that happened for our fishermen. We knew the price before catching and more important, instead of counting out the fish from the boat, all palagic fish were scooped into baskets and weighed. It became very much easier and quicker to land and we were paid for what was landed. With palagic fish however, for every one hundred stone landed, there was an agreed amount given over to the buyer to make up for any broken fish. In the main this worked very well, but the fact that the control prices had not been readjusted for some years did finally cause very much resentment among fishermen. Eventually the controls were lifted and fish was sold on the open market, at least the white fish was, but pilchards were sold under contract by agreement to the various processors of canning or salting. As the demand for pilchards increased, the Ministry of Agriculture and Fisheries tried to encourage our Cornish fishermen to try other methods of catching besides the drift net. A Scottish fishing boat was engaged fitted with the ring net method to come down into our Cornish waters to show us how to improve our catching potential. It was proved that it was possible to catch many more pilchards in the ring net at certain times, but it was subject however, to the fish being in concentrated shoals as in the winter time. Also weather conditions had to be moderate for handling the fishing gear. The most important factor against this fishing was that both the ring net and the purse seine net were catching all sizes and the fish scales, that made the fish look so nice when packed into barrels, were rubbed off through the catch being jammed tightly in the confined space of these nets. Both methods of fishing were condemned even after several of our Cornish boats went to the expense of buying the gear. The pilchard curers demanded not only fish with scales but also of a regular size for packing. The uniform size was also required because the heading and gutting machines were set to accept a certain length of fish. The pilchards passed through the machine on a conveyor belt and if they were too long there was wastage but if they were too short either the head or tail would not be cut off at all. Fish other than the size required by the machine had to be cut by hand and this proved too costly and impracticable. The only method of ensuring catching fish of a uniform size was with the drift net of a certain mesh which would allow the smaller ones to escape while the very large fish would not become enmeshed.

In 1948 the Cornish pilchard fleet increased to approximately 160 boats, manned by 600 men and as the demand grew our Looe fleet also increased. We found that the mesh size we were using during the summer months was too small. The shoals of larger pilchards were considered to be breeders and usually remained farther off in the

Two sides of the coin. Above Skipper Alfred Sammels of the lugger I.R.I.S. *knee deep in pilchards with a splendid catch while below fish being dumped in the sea because there was more caught than the canners required for that day.*

channel. Because they began making their appearance closer in shore and because by this time the fish were being sold by weight and not by numbers our fishermen were forced to buy nets of larger mesh but the price had risen rapidly.

As it happened at this time there were many herring nets for sale at Lowestoft and Yarmouth. The steam drifters had suffered a serious recession at this time because of the introduction of the deep water trawl and the consequent depletion of the herring stocks in the North Sea. We were thus able to buy several of the drift nets with the larger mesh which they had been using and which were very suitable for our requirements. The Lowestoft nets had ropes along the top heavily corked, with a heavy rope along the bottom or skirt and they were very much shorter than ours. We cut off the top rope, turned the net upside down by putting the corks into what had been the footrope and we then joined four together making a long net of 120 yards. It takes about 15 nets of this length joined together to make up one fleet of nets each boat used in fishing.

The large shed which had been used in the building of the M.L.s during the war was now taken over and turned into a canning factory. The firm, known as Cornish Products, was able to process a large quantity of fish and in addition to taking the catches from our Looe boats it also absorbed much of that landed by Polperro craft and even some from as far afield as Porthleven. At this time pilchards were priced at 4/6d. per stone and added to this the Ministry paid another 10d. by way of a subsidy to help in the running costs.

In the early 1950s some of the boats installed echo sounding equipment to locate the shoals, which proved of tremendous value and increased the catching potential of the boats enormously. The element of chance was very much eliminated as it not only finds the shoal but it also gives its depth. For bottom fishing it gives the contour of the sea bed and the depth of water below the vessel which is a most valuable aid in foggy weather for navigation. With such a large fleet of drifters, trawlers, long liners and crabbers being built up in Cornwall the future looked bright and full of promise and many fishermen obtained loans or grants from the Government for new craft. 1956 saw fine catches of pilchards which fetched good prices but this very same year was to witness the end of the Cornish pilchard industry as we knew it.

American canners had put up huge factories in South Africa and with the cheap labour there plus the abundance of pilchard shoals that had not been exploited it was possible to make huge catches of fish with the big encircling nets working from larger boats. The bulk of this was taken for fish meal and oil extraction with the remainder being used for canning. When unloading the fish from the boats it was sucked out by large hosepipes and motor pumps. Canned pilchards were dumped in this country at lower prices than our fish could be caught and processed. Although our Cornish canned fish were of better quality the housewife not unnaturally bought the cheaper South African cans. In 1956 12,000 tons of canned pilchards were imported into this country. In the next few years the price of our fish had to drop as the demand grew less and canners were soon driven out of business as they could not compete.

A two year research project was carried out by the White Fish Authority using a large craft fitted out with the most up-to-date equipment for finding and catching pilchards which the scientists reported must be there. Quite a lot of money was spent in the experiment the object of which was to prove to us Cornish fishermen that more could be caught with bigger boats and the latest gear. It was hoped that larger catches would result in cheaper landing prices and thus allow the canners sufficient profit to be able to compete with the imported variety and stay in business. Before the project started we were asked for our opinion and we advised against it being carried out. Men do not spend a lifetime at a certain job without knowing at least some of the sort of things one can or cannot do in that particular field. The whole experiment was a failure and did not do anything to halt the decline in the Cornish pilchard industry.

So many canners went out of business that during the summers of 1959 and 1960 although only five boats were drift net fishing from Looe we were often bringing in to port hundreds of stones of pilchards more than was required by the only canner left. No one could forecast just how much fish would be caught on any particular night but after satisfying the canner's demand of 800 stone the rest had to be dumped back in the sea. It was a heartbreaking and demoralising job to do this after a hard night at sea and yet on some other occasions there was not enough brought in to supply the canner's needs. In order to help the few men and boats left to have an equal share of the proceeds we agreed to land a certain number of stones of fish from each boat according to the number in the crew. It soon became clear to us that with the restricted landings and the fall in price of pilchards to 3/3d. or 3/6d. per stone there just was not enough earnings for us to carry on for long. Added to this our winter drift net fishing had failed almost completely. Many boats were sold and most of the young men left although as many had previously learnt other trades they were able to find some employment. The few of us left had to lay up our boats in winter and sign on the Labour Exchange..

A heavy catch aboard Our Daddy *in April 1964. The crew are shaking pilchards out of the net which is stowed forward as it is cleaned out. The larger spar across the boat is the roller which is fitted to the starboard rail of the bulwarks when hauling in nets at sea. In the lower picture the net room can be seen.*

DRIFT NET Looe Specification

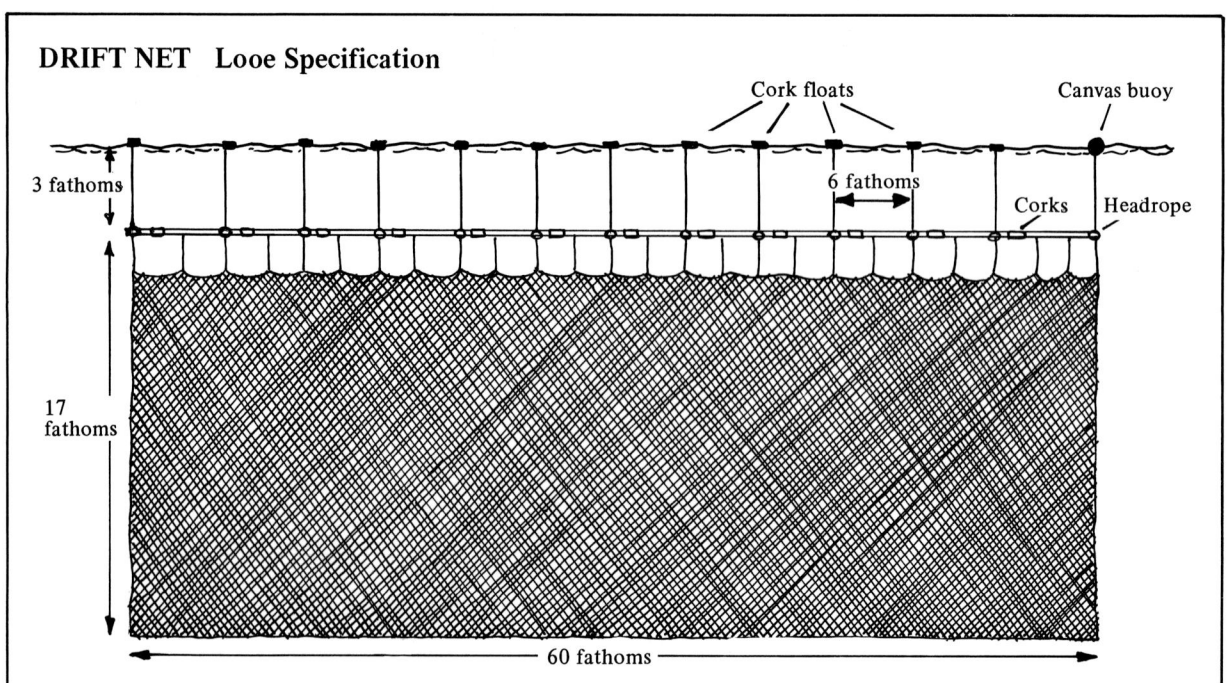

Labels: Cork floats, Canvas buoy, 6 fathoms, Corks, Headrope, 3 fathoms, 17 fathoms, 60 fathoms

Diagram of a drift net as used by the Looe boats during the summer season, up to fifteen nets would be joined end on together, each net 60 fathoms in length, to give a full fleet of nets, a little more than a mile of nets. In the winter an average of 10 nets at 60 fathoms each.

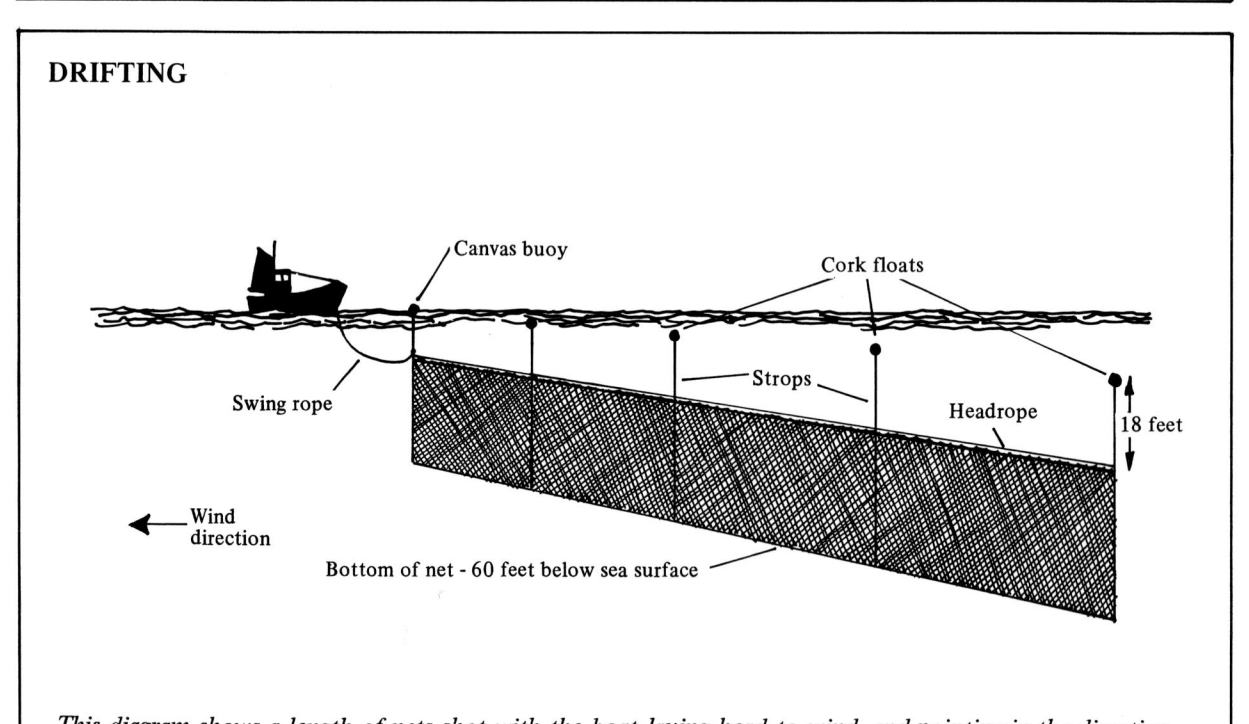

DRIFTING

Labels: Canvas buoy, Cork floats, Strops, Headrope, 18 feet, Swing rope, Wind direction, Bottom of net - 60 feet below sea surface

This diagram shows a length of nets shot with the boat laying head to wind, and pointing in the direction of the nets with the rope attached, known as the swing rope.

LONG LINING

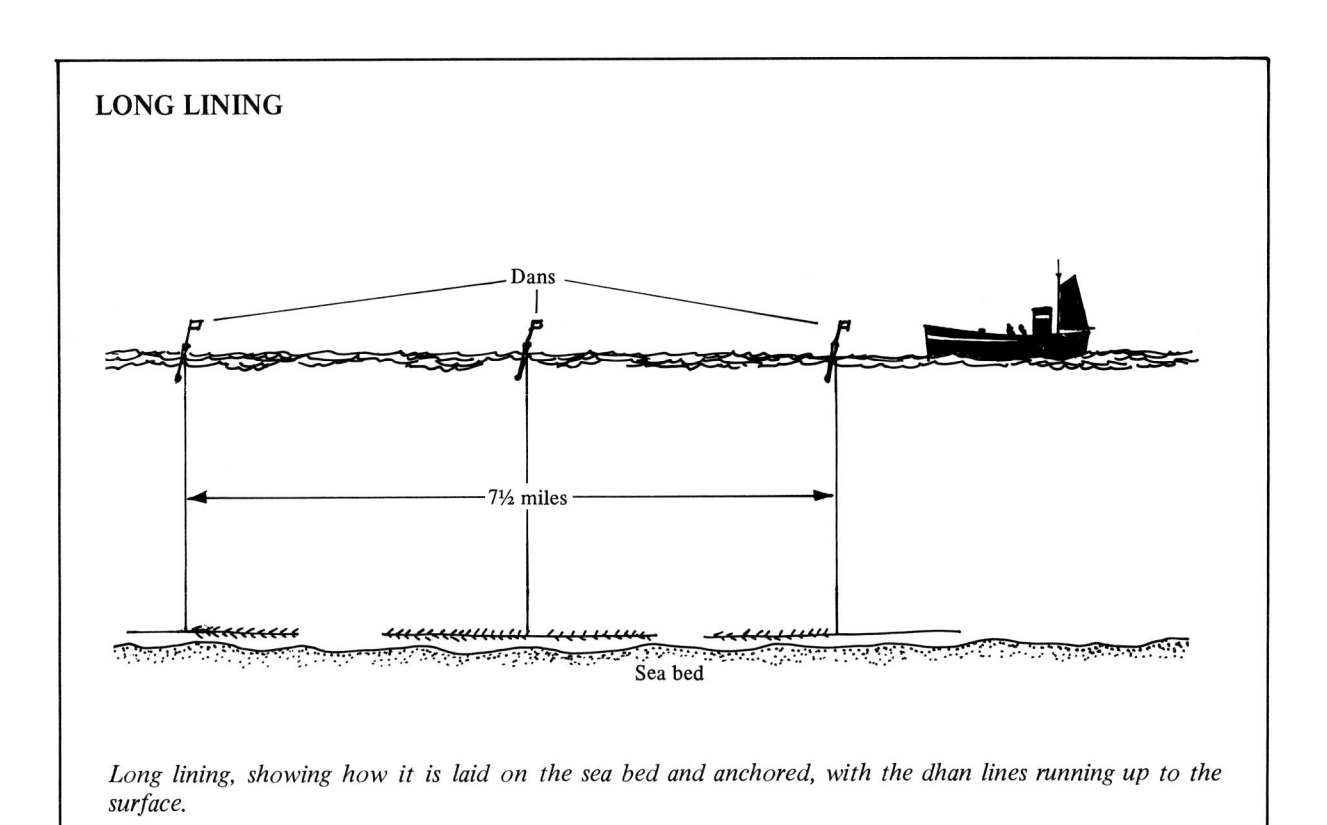

Long lining, showing how it is laid on the sea bed and anchored, with the dhan lines running up to the surface.

TRAWLING

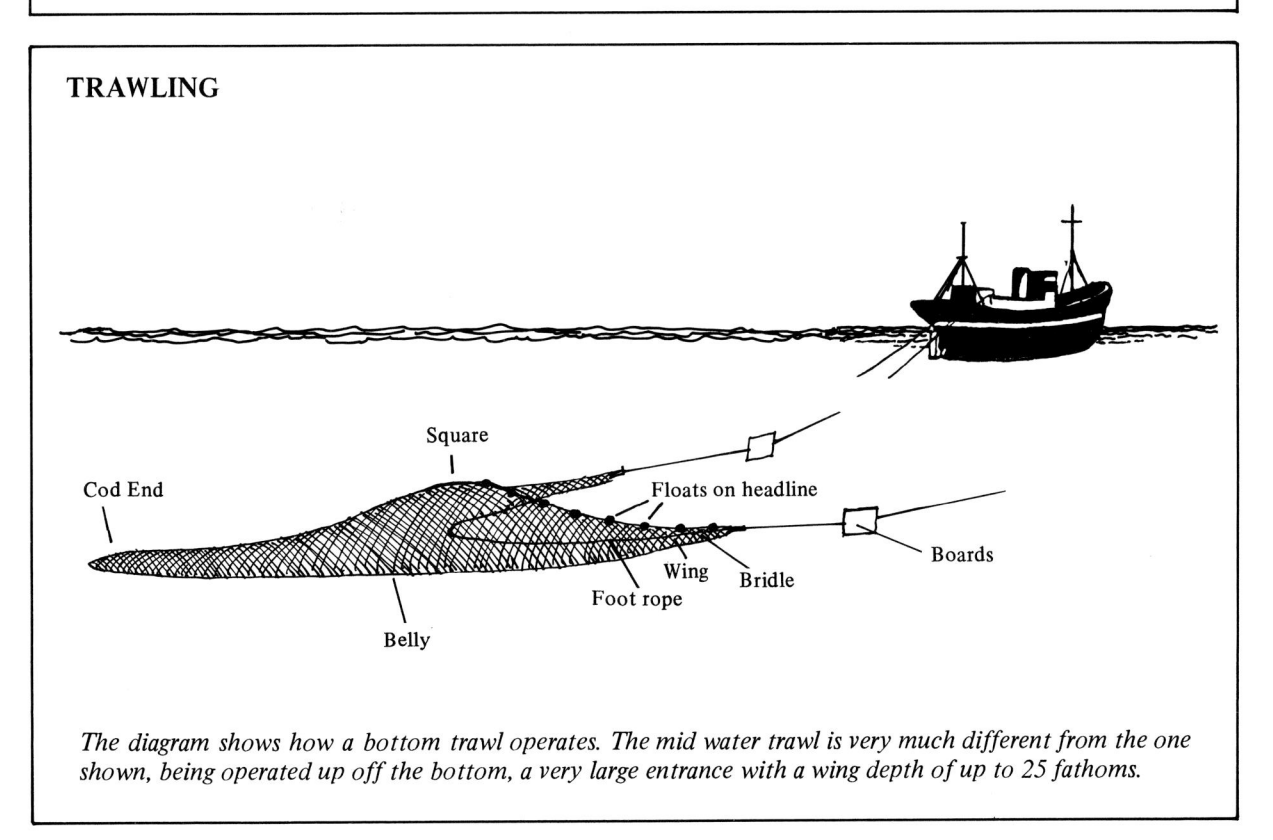

The diagram shows how a bottom trawl operates. The mid water trawl is very much different from the one shown, being operated up off the bottom, a very large entrance with a wing depth of up to 25 fathoms.

Alfred Pengelly and a crew member unloading, weighing and boxing the catch.

Fish laid out on the quay ready for the buyers.

Cleaning dogfish on the quayside at Looe, sold in the shops as rock salmon.

Drying the 'long lines' at the end of the season. In this photograph are Alfred Pengelly, his father, grandfather and uncle.

A. J. Pengelly supervising the drying of the drift nets.

Nets piled on the quay for barking, ready to be dipped in the hot cutch.

83

Pat, of the Jolly Roger Shark Angling Club, London, has hooked a shark. The boat is lying with engines stopped, broadside to wind. To attract the sharks some net bags of mashed pilchards or mackerel are lowered over the side and shaken about at intervals. With the boat blowing away, broadside to wind, gradually a strong trail of fishy water is laid, known as rubby dubby. The lines with baited hooks are trailing away in this stream with a cork float attached to allow the bait to drop a certain distance below the surface.

The shark angler sits in a large swivel chair with the bottom of the rod resting in a special fitting for support and easier handling. The blue shark being brought on board is about 60 lb. Sometimes in a fresh wind with a heavy fish hooked the engines are started and the boat moved gently into the wind to ease the strain on the line.

THE SHARK FISHING AND PLEASURE TRADE EXPANDS.

One interesting and helpful change taking place during the periods of depression in the post war Cornish fishing industry was the increasing number of people spending their holidays in the county. Some of our smaller boats were enagaged in taking out parties during the summer on fishing trips etc, then laying up their boats in the winter and coming on shore to work. It was also during this time that a retired Army Brigadier named Caunter, who lived in Looe, had for some time been shark fishing for the sport of it, also encouraging his friends to join him. This soon became generally popular, so much so that boats were being hired to take more people out to sea on these expeditions. The fishing became competitive among anglers and eventually a shark angling club was formed in Looe, known as "The Shark Angling Club of Great Britain". Its success was, and still is, tremendous. The founder, Brigadier J. L. Caunter, should always be remembered with grateful thanks by all who have benefitted both financially with their boats and by all who have derived great pleasure in the sport.

It became so popular that there were not enough boats for the number of people wanting to have a go, so eventually we fitted out our luggers. There were only five big boats left in the port at this time, in the commercial fishing, drifting. We did drift net fishing through the night, landing our agreed amount of pilchards in the morning, then cleaned up the boat, and at 9.00 a.m. two of the crew would take a certain number of people out for the day shark fishing, getting back in harbour about 6.00 p.m. to land. The other members of the crew would rejoin the boat then for the night's drift net fishing. Next morning, two other crew members would take the boat out with people and this went on all through the summer season. With only a crew of four all told, it was a very tiring experience. We were, however, glad to do this extra work in the summer to help us over the winter months. We tried long lining in the winter but weather conditions and bait problems etc., made this a very hazardous job. During the Spring of 1965, my uncle, who had been my partner in the *Our Daddy,* died. He had been on shore, retired for nine years, and I bought his share of the boat from my Aunt, so now for the first time I became owner of my own boat. At this time in the fishing it was a gamble to take on a Bank loan at the age of sixty and endeavour to get a living out of a fishing boat. It had, however, been my life's work and I accepted the challenge eagerly. In the autumn of that year, five boats from Looe, including my own, fitted out with mackerel feather fishing equipment on hand lines. We joined up with some boats from Mevagissey who were similarly equipped and had been having some success in this field. It was not a new fishing to us, as we had done one or two seasons directly after the war with the same gear, but at that time the German trawlers had spoilt the fishing for us. These very large deep sea vessels would lay quiet all through the day, then towards evening they would shoot their midwater trawls and tear through the shoals of mackerel. All the night through this kind of intensive fishing soon broke up the shoals and in a very short time our mackerel hand line fishing was gone. For many winter seasons after this there was little to be earned. Several years later our Government introduced a twelve mile fishing limit that kept all foreign craft outside this, except those that had traditionally fished close to our shores, such as the Belgian and French. So the German, Polish and Russian craft were barred from fishing inside of 12 miles while the French and Belgian vessels were not allowed within six miles. There is no doubt that by 1966 we saw the benefit of these extended limits and it had allowed the palagic stock such as mackerel to build up. In the winter of 1966, for the first time in years, we were able to secure a very good living with the season commencing in late September and carrying on until the end of March in the following year.

Again in the summer we fitted our boats for drift net fishing for pilchards at night and shark fishing by day with the visitors. The following winter saw more boats joining the fleet for mackerel fishing. Some of the smaller boats that had previously been laid up after the shark angling season were now fitted out for fishing instead of the crew working on shore. It is certain that our young men would rather fish for a living as it is quite a different kind of life and our men are always willing to accept a challenge of this nature. Men are forced out of their boats only when a living is not to be had at sea, so once again conditions began to improve. During these first three winter seasons, the mackerel fishing was carried on fairly close between two and six miles of the coast. This allowed the smaller boats from our South coast ports to take part in it and more men and boats joined the fleets each season. During February 1969, my eldest son, Terry, who had been working on shore as a carpenter and builder since leaving school, quite out of the blue, suddenly decided that he would come fishing with me in *Our Daddy.* Leaving a well-paid job and with a wife and two children to support, I felt a little uneasy as to whether it was the right thing to do or not, knowing the uncertainties in the life of a fisherman with all its ups and downs. I was also pleased in a way to realise and hope, that perhaps one day, if all went well, he would take on where I left off, as I had been able to do with my own father, thus to preserve the family traditions handed down for many generations.

The winter mackerel seasons improved but, on the other hand, the summer pilchard fishery declined to such an extent that very few boats in Cornwall were engaged in it. Whereas in 1948 there were about 600 men and 160 boats engaged in the Cornish pilchard fishery, by 1967 there were fewer than 50 men and less than 10 boats regularly employed. This I am afraid is a sad story and I can see no happy ending as far as Cornish fishermen are concerned. What with the serious exploitation of stock by the larger craft for fish meal, plus the important factor that foreign imported canned pilchards are cheaper than we can produce, seems to have condemned to death what used to be Cornwall's greatest fish producing asset. I remember with nostalgia the many seasons when there was a large Cornish fleet of boats and the many friends who took part together, from the various ports, in their search for fish.

I gave up the summer pilchard fishing as a bad job in the late sixties and son Terry and I fitted out the boat for shark fishing only during the summer months. We are equipped with all the necessary gear with six heavy shark rods and six small rods to cater for twelve people fishing at one time. Every half an hour these people take turns on the different rods so that everyone has the chance to catch a shark providing of course, the luck goes with them. On the smaller rods, it is mackerel fishing or ground fishing for whiting. This is very popular and to people on holiday from factories or offices is a wonderful relaxation, besides giving them a sport that some of them have never experienced before. The Shark Angling Club of Great Britain provides trophies and other prizes to be won by its members throughout the season. Both angler and skipper of the boat, catching the largest specimen shark or the most qualifying sharks at 75 lb. and over, are eligible. To become a member of the Club one has to catch a shark of 75 lb. but prizes are awarded for the different kind of shark caught and the tackle used in catching, so all in all it is good fun. With more than twenty boats engaged in this kind of fishing all through the summer months it ensures a very good living for the boatmen during this period of time when there seems little prospects of so many boats and men being able to earn a living at commercial fishing.

When the summer ends one or two more hands are taken on as crew members and the boat is once again fitted out for the winter season. The technique in the mackerel fishing itself had improved considerably in a few years, so much so that catches were increased three to four hundred per cent. With the echo sounding equipment we could find the shoals of fish and sometimes a very small mark on the indicator paper would put us on to a good bit of fishing. Many boats were also equipped with wireless transmitters.

It became a general practice when the boats went to sea early in the morning from the various ports along the south Cornish coast, to contact one another to find out what the fishing was like and to try and determine the best area to work from that day, that is of course, unless it happened to be a very long way to steam. The fishing gear was improved also. In the early days of mackerel fishing we used hand lines and seldom fished below twenty fathoms with a gut trace of some twelve to fifteen hooks with coloured feathers attached which attracted the fish. There was a lead weight on the bottom end of the trace of about 1½ lb. to pull it down. A catch of 100 stone of mackerel was considered to be a very good day. The echo sounding proved to us that at times the fish were very much deeper even close to the sea bed at 30 and 40 fathoms down. It became common to fish at these depths and very often the larger mackerel would be found down there. We had hand winches made up to fit on the rail of the boat, so instead of hauling the line by hand it could be wound up on a large reel, thus saving a lot of time. It was possible to use a three pound lead on the bottom of the mackerel trace with 28 to 35 hooks spaced about nine inches apart. The weight of the lead would pull the line down off the reel. The hooks are now covered with coloured plastic tubing instead of feathers which quickly wore out in good fishing. With the use of so many more hooks and much stronger gut traces it is not uncommon during the winter fishing for a three man crew to bring into port three to four hundred stone of mackerel on a certain day's fishing.

The idea of the winch for mackerel fishing was first introduced at Looe during the last war for whiting fishing. Not only was it a faster way of bringing the line up, but the line, being tightly wound on the reel or gurdy as it is now called, keeps it always clear and ready for use. When previously pulling the line up by hand on to the deck in fresh winds it would tend to tangle up, even more so, if there were a lot of mackerel kicking around the deck. When we started to use these winches on our boats, some of the fishermen from the other Westcountry ports began to find out when working with us, that they were being outfished considerably and because of this we were able to land more fish per crew member in a day's fishing in the same shoal.

One day, a boat from Mevagissey came alongside us and timed his crew against mine in handling the mackerel line. It was not long before he ordered the same equipment as we had. On another occasion the skipper of the boat *Cour de Lion* from Porthleven, Charlie Laiety, who had been fishing in company with us all through the day came over to me on his radio. He said, "Alfred, I am coming into port with you tonight, I want to see what sort of gear you are using". "Right you are, Charlie", I replied, "you are welcome". We came into port with the *Cour de Lion* close behind. We moored up the boats and landed the catches and then, sure enough, Charlie with his son Bobby

Running for harbour in a fresh wind with seas breaking astern. The canvas shelter is a portable structure used for passengers in the sharking season.

Our Daddy *entering harbour on a fine day after a sharking trip. A yellow pennant above a blue denotes a shark caught.*

came on board, inspected our hand winches and ordered one for each member of his crew. There is no doubt that as this method of fishing spread through the Cornish fleet, the landings of mackerel improved considerably in all the Cornish ports.

One very important thing when mackerel fishing, is to try to determine in what direction the fish are heading. Sometimes the swim is against the tide which we call 'stemming the tide', while at other times, with a moderate or fresh wind, the mackerel will swim into the wind. This may happen very often with a fresh on-shore breeze so it is the skipper's job, when fishing, to try and work out this problem. At times he has to keep his boat pointing straight into the wind. To help steer the boat, the mizzen sail has to be set with the sheet of the sail hauled into the centre of the stern tightly, the wind force then on the sail will do more good in steering than the rudder itself. With the engine in forward gear gently pushing the boat ahead and the fishing lines trailing slightly aft, the boat can go along with the shoal. The crew are spread out along the deck from bow to stern fishing and the skipper has to keep his eye on how each man is faring. If the chap at the bow is most successful it may pay to go a little ahead and place the ship more over the shoal. If the stern man is getting better results it may be worthwhile to drop back. At other times it may be found to be better with the boat just laying broadside to the wind allowing it to blow away and so to remain in a shoal of fish that are dropping to leeward or swimming with the wind. All these kinds of different situations in mackerel fishing make it more interesting and become a challenge to the skipper and crew of a boat. It is certain that if a skipper can keep his boat pointing or drifting in the same direction as the shoal of fish is heading, then longer fishing time can be had, very often with less steaming time spent in searching around for the shoal of fish. Sometimes there may be a number of boats concentrating on the same shoal of fish working quite close together and often on a very fine day one can almost jump from one boat to another. At such times as this, all eyes are looking for the boat that has the best fishing. When this is determined, all hands make a beeline to get one side or other of this boat. Usually, however, it is not very long before the boats are on the move again as a lot of craft in a small area will very often upset the fishing and the shoal may disperse. These things very often depend on the size of the shoal of fish and perhaps weather conditions, but as I have already stated, the fisherman is not yet born who can predetermine the movements of palagic fish. With experience, however, over the years, fishing in certain areas, one can hazard a very good guess and I always maintain that 'fishing is a glorious uncertainty'.

The different seasons in fishing come and go each year, some bad, some good. In the bad times when all seems lost and many give up the job, perhaps another kind of fishing has come along to encourage those that are left to carry on in the hope of better things to come. I have witnessed very many changes in the life of our inshore fishermen over this last half a century. A fisherman has to have a deep faith in his calling and be dedicated to it but time spent in maintaining and looking after a boat and all its equipment and fishing gear whilst in harbour is all important to success. It is always said that there is also a lot of luck and this is perhaps true. But it is also true to say that a fisherman who has had good training at sea and has the very best equipment is the one most likely to get the luck.

At this time of writing, July 1974, I am on shore for the first summer since 1920. My son Terry, is now skipper of *Our Daddy* with another hand as crew, and they are at sea with a number of visitors on a shark fishing trip. Had anyone told me many years ago that I would be engaged with my boat in this kind of fishing, I would never have believed them as at that time it was not even thought about. Force of circumstances, however, in the fishing industry induced many of us to do this catering for the visitors and it is in many ways a welcome change. The boats are painted up and kept clean all summer and there is not the worry of having to punish yourself or the boat in bad weather and we make many friends who will often come back again for a trip to sea. It does not seem, looking back over the years, that the blue shark was very much in evidence in our part of the English Channel at any time of the year. Between the 1914-18 to 1939-45 wars, we had no summer pilchard season off Looe during that time, even so, when fishing off the Mounts Bay with drift nets during the summer season there was little evidence to prove that there were any blue sharks in numbers in that area either. Our fleet of drift nets were in the sea sometimes all through the night hours whilst the crews were hauling and shaking the fish out of the nets on to the decks, and had there been sharks around, much damage would have been done to the nets. It was a different story after the last war, when the pilchard shoals returned in the summer months to our part of the Cornish coast, and many blue sharks came up the Channel. So much did the shark increase that all along the south Cornish coast, from the Wolf Rock to the Eddystone Lighthouse area, that it was a very risky operation to put drift nets into the sea for pilchards, except close inshore. The shark was capable of causing great damage to the nets, many being ruined beyond repair. It is considered that sea temperatures had become warmer during these later years, during the summer months, because a part of the Gulf Stream finds its way up the English Channel, thus bringing the blue shark in its warmer sea water. It would seem, however, that we are only on the eastern edge of this movement of current as the blue shark does not reach very far up off the Devon coast. These fish arrive in early June and are gone again during October. It seems also that the amount of sharks and the time or dates of arrival is governed very much by the preceding winter weather, be it a severely cold or a mild winter. Some of the best shark fishing has been had so far this present summer, after one of the mildest winters for a long time. The shark angling is, of course, competitive, one is always hoping for the largest fish to satisfy the customer. Financially however, the catch is on board for skipper and crew before leaving harbour which is of a great help.

It has been said by some people that shark angling is a cruel sport. From ten years experience in sharking and from a study of statistics on the subject I would not agree. It differs very little from other kinds of fishing in this respect, except for the savagery of the fish itself when being handled and what it would do to you if you were not careful. By far the largest percentage of sharks caught are carefully unhooked and returned to the sea to swim again. Hundreds are tagged with a small plastic disc bearing a number. The skipper carries out this minor operation by fastening it on the dorsal fin with a special instrument supplied by the Marine Biological Association, Plymouth, who are making a study of the movements of the blue shark in the sea areas from our shores down into the Atlantic. It has now been reported by the above association that a blue shark caught, tagged and released off Falmouth in 1972 by Mr. R. Vinnicombe has recently been caught again by a Japanese long line fishing vessel some 2,000 miles out in the Atlantic. During the year 1974 some 630 sharks were tagged and eight recaptures made bringing the total to 16 returns from 1,560 sharks marked. This return rate of 1% is very encouraging from a migratory fish and it suggests that almost all the sharks tagged are still surviving. From the results obtained so far it is possible to make some general observations.

It seems that sharks leave our coasts about the end of September although some larger ones may remain a little longer. In the area of Northern Spain they may remain as late as November after which they move south to the Canary Islands with this migration being reversed in the spring. Recaptures of Portuguese tagged fish suggest that very small blues tend to remain within a relatively restricted area farther south and most do not take part in the northerly migration to our coast until about their third year. Growth rates from tag returns in general support observations on age determination from vertebral rings which indicate that blue sharks grow about 30cm a year. Here are the recaptures made in 1974 which illustrate the trends.

No. 330 (orange)   Tagged April 24th 1974 at Sagres, Portugal by Mr. W. Persoon.
                   Recaptured July 26th 1974 off Setubal, Portugal.

No. 561 (green)   Tagged June 12th 1973 at Looe by Mr. T. Pengelly.
                   Recaptured July 15th 1974 off Ile d'Yeu, France.

No. 1322 (green)   Tagged July 23rd 1974 at Looe by Mr. Bill Cowan.
                   Recaptured August 26th 1974 at Looe by R. Butters, Jnr.

No. 88 (orange)   Tagged September 5th 1973 at Sagres by Mr. W. Persoon.
                   Recaptured September 13th 1974 off Cape Espichel, Portugal.

No. 1405 (green)   Tagged August 22nd 1974 at Looe by Mr. Bill Cowan.
                   Recaptured September 24th 1974 near Cape Finisterre, Spain.

No. 650 (green)   Tagged August 20th 1974 at Falmouth by Mr. C. MacGillivray.
                   Recaptured September 15th 1974 off Gijon, Spain.

No. 1127 (green)   Tagged July 31st 1974 at Looe by Mr. R. Butters, Jnr.
                   Recaptured November 14th 1974 off La Coruna, Spain.

No. 83 (red)   Tagged August 17th 1974 at Newquay by Mr. R. Eglinton.
                   Recaptured November 8th 1974 off La Coruna, Spain.

	1971	1972	1973	1974	1975	1976	1977
Sharks caught from Looe	4087	1659	2567	3060	2083	928	806
Sharks weighed at Looe	429	372	334	518	398	279	225
Sharks over 75 lbs. at Looe	195	155	98	222	182	103	90

Another satisfied customer on Our Daddy. *He has caught a shark of 86 lbs. which qualifies him for membership of the Shark Angling Club of Great Britain;*

The new member with his shark at the weighing station and very proud he looks.

MARKETING THE CATCH.

As I have previously stated, after many bad winter seasons 1966 was the first that it had been really worthwhile taking part in any palagic fishing in order to make a living. During the later part of the summer pilchard season we had been catching a few stones of mackerel also each night in the drift nets. The whole of the catch from the few Looe boats operating at the time was being transported to Newlyn where the pilchards were being handed over to a processing firm. The mackerel was taken to one of the best known fresh fish buyers and fetched a very satisfactory price.

When the pilchards season ended in early October we were encouraged by the Newlyn Merchant to fish entirely for mackerel with hand lines during the following winter months. Five boats from Looe, including my own, fitted out with the necessary fishing gear and we joined with boats from Mevagissey making a small fleet fishing all day and landing the catch in the evening. The fish was then transported to the Newlyn man for packing and sending to the inland markets where all went well with very good prices obtained. It was very pleasant for the few of us left in the fishing at that time to know that it was possible to earn one's living again at the job we were brought up to do.

Soon many more boats joined the fleet with a mackerel packing station set up in Looe by the same Newlyn firm. One or two more buyers came into the trade and to supply them fleets of boats began to build up in all the Cornish ports. By 1968/69 the Cornish mackerel fleet was considerable and had overreached itself with catching capacity exceeding the marketing requirements. This meant that landings had to be controlled and many times considerably curtailed. The demand was limited almost entirely to our English markets and it was considered at the time that the total daily need was in the region of two or three thousand stone. Many times the boats were only allowed to land 25 to 30 stone of mackerel per each member of the crew with no small fish at all and only a limited amount of medium size. On those days it meant many stones of the smaller fish had to be dumped back into the sea. It became evident that a very much larger outlet for mackerel had to be found and this sentiment was expressed throughout all the Cornish fishing fleets.

During the summer of 1971 a meeting was held at Newlyn for all Cornish fishermen with the idea of forming a co-operative society. Men from most of the ports agreed to its formation as we had little time to lose because of the restricted landings. Boats from Newlyn, St. Ives, Padstow, Porthleven, Falmouth, Polperro and Looe joined and set up the co-op which was given the title Cornish Fishermen Limited or C.F.L. The boats from Mevagissey did not join as they had their own co-operative already in operation. Sad to relate our company got off to a bad start as very short of capital, and with management problems plus other reasons best not mentioned, it never really got off the ground. It must be said however, that the Committee persevered and worked hard to save the organisation and great credit is due to the early members.

The Brixham Trawlers Federation was called in to help as its success in running a similar scheme was well known. It was finally agreed that they should take over all the sales of the fish from the C.F.L. This idea worked well and in fact it was the first time that the Brixham Co-op had taken part in marketing mackerel in a big way. Markets were found across the channel in France, Germany, Holland and other outlets and these expanded rapidly during the second and third seasons of operations, with hundreds of tons of fish being deep frozen and shipped across. The winter of 1974/75 saw an increase in the landings of larger size mackerel and still more boats joined the fleets in the various Cornish harbours. I think Falmouth had the largest influx of fishing craft during those winters and a part of its fleet formed their own Co-op to trade direct with a French fish merchant.

The Co-op packing station at Looe, which is managed incidently by my second son, David with his wife Diana as secretary, is handling mackerel from thirty boats including some from Polperro and Fowey. On most occasions the fish are caught, landed, packed and away to their destinations on the same day. On one day six thousand stone of mackerel were packed and ready for transport by 8.30 p.m. and the following day with boats landing their catch from 4.30 p.m. onwards, no less than seven thousand stone had been despatched by 9.30 p.m. All are in two-stone cardboard boxes for which casual labour is employed and all the boxes are made up at the packing station from cardboard sheets precut to size and shape and fastened with wire staples by a small hand operated machine. Each boat's catch, already sorted by the crew into four sizes (large, large/medium, medium, small) is weighed into boxes, iced and stacked on wood pallets each holding 160 stone or one ton.

The fish are handled in turn starting with the large variety and so on and all are packed according to size on the pallets and then loaded into container lorries by fork-lift truck. It takes little time to fill a twenty ton lorry by this method. Throughout the night the lorries are on their way to markets or deep freezer plants up country where they are held until required while the Roscoff Ferry is much used for consignments to the Continent. It is estimated that about 80% of our catches of mackerel finds its way across the channel to places ranging from Sweden right down the coast to France, and this demand is increasing. Catching, landing, packing and transporting mackerel is taking place in other Cornish ports such as Newlyn, Falmouth and Mevagissey while the Polperro boats pack their own and then bring it to Looe to be added to our scheme and marketed through our co-operative. In the winter season 1973/74, 121,000 stone of mackerel caught by the Looe and Polperro fleets was despatched from Looe. In the following winter to 12th January no less than 170,000 stone had been landed in the two ports. This was the heaviest amount for three seasons and the fishing usually continues through to March.

An entirely new situation has now arisen in the marketing of fish. The European Economic Community had had a minimum price scheme for some time whereby groups of fishermen can form what is known as a Fish Producer Organisation which has to be properly constituted and registered with rules and regulations acceptable to and recognised by the Ministry of Agriculture and Fisheries also the E.E.C. minimum price requirements. Such an organisation has been set up in the south west known as the South Western Fish Producer Organisation Ltd. All boats trading to both the Brixham Trawlers Federation and the Cornish Fishermens Ltd are members and also some other boats outside the two co-operatives, but it is entirely optional to join. The Organisation states minimum prices for fish at first hand sale and if prices offered are below this figure the fish are withdrawn. If it is in good condition it is then transported to fish meal plants and a small price paid for it. For each boat's withdrawn fish records are passed to the Ministry whose representatives inspect the withdrawn catches. Later on a subsidy drawn from Community funds in Brussels makes up the difference to fishermen to a guaranteed amount.

As far as Cornish hand line fishermen are concerned the scheme affects the medium and small size mackerel which meet a limited demand on the market when there are heavy landings. It has encouraged more intensive fishing with the knowledge that past conditions of having to dump unwanted small and medium mackerel back into the sea no longer exists. There is always a good demand for the larger fish and their sale presents no problem. For boats trading through the Producers Organisation it is now possible to fish ad lib throughout the winter season even with such large fleets operating over the shoals. The only control on amounts of landing now are caused either by temporary lack of sufficient transport or deep freezing facilities. Should any man ask me, "Would you join the Common Market?", I am bound to reply without any political prejudice, "Brother we have been in it for some time". Our livelihood as fishermen depends on the continental markets very much indeed. We are not however, too happy with the thought that we have to hand over fresh mackerel to fish meal plants when in many countries throughout the world people are starving.

As the pattern of commercial fishing changes over the years and new techniques in locating and catching are introduced, particularly in palagic fishing the new generation of fishermen may never know, unless handed down by their elders, the signs and methods evolved in the past by instinct and practice. Nature provided many of these indications but modern electronic aids take little notice of these. I have found, however, that if one has an idea of what to look for regarding bird movements etc, the conclusions one comes to for fish finding are often merely confirmed by the echo sounder.

There is forever in the minds of inshore fishermen a fear that the grounds and stocks of fish in coastal areas will become exploited and depleted by the intensive fishing by large craft. The big boats using the mid water trawl have already so depleted the pilchard stocks that it is now almost finished as an economic viability and now they are turning their attention to the mackerel. It was recently estimated that on one night's fishing just three trawlers landed 180 tons, and at this rate it may not be long before the mackerel are gone also. If this continues the fisherman's fear of catching beating breeding may become a reality.

Another lorry load of mackerel packed in two-stone cardboard boxes ready to leave the quayside at Looe.

Scenes while unloading on to the quay all washed and sorted in size. On top of each tray is a label with the name of the boat and the grade of fish.

Night work on the mackerel catch at Looe. Above: Unloading on to the Quay. Below: In the packing station, weighing and placing in the two-stone cardboard boxes.

IN CONCLUSION.

Our Daddy served my family well, in fair winds and foul, and the crews that sailed in her and still do, with Bill Wadling now skipper, carrying out the job she was built for in 1921, to catch fish. We have travelled thousands of miles and landed countless tons of fish. Many times we have been caught out in gales particularly early in the year when long line fishing some 60 miles off shore. It's always a six hour job to get the seven miles of line on board before starting the long journey home. It was a very rare occurance for any of our boats to leave the line and run for shelter when caught in a storm. Luckily I have never had to do this. As long as the engines will tick over and the mizzen is set aft to steady her it is wonderful what these little ships will stand up to and come through. I have had more anxious times coming in from the Channel, crossing the shipping lanes in fog than I have experienced in bad weather. Over the years one acquires a deep respect for the sea which enables you to known when and when not to put to sea no matter how big your craft. There is something out there much more powerful than man or his frail ships and if you are forced to learn this the hard way then 'may heaven help you'.

Of course when asked if I have ever been caught out at sea in a gale my answer must be, "Yes", for how could anyone spend more than half a century fishing and yet escape all the winds that blow. One or two instances come to mind. It was in early April 1948 and we had been at sea for most of the night shooting and hauling drift nets to catch pilchard for baiting long lines. Almost 2,000 fish are needed for this and sometimes boats would catch enough early in the evening and then carry on full speed to the fishing grounds way out in the Channel. On this occasion we returned to harbour and had a few hours rest and then left harbour the next day after lunch intending to shoot the long line that evening. We headed for the Eddystone and then set course 35 miles S.S.E. from the lighthouse in order to shoot just before dark. As we steamed we cut up the pilchards and baited the hooks which are secured to the line on 3 ft. strops set about 9 ft. apart. The lines are stowed in fairly large round baskets with the baited hooks hanging around the topsides. As each basket of line is fed out and emptied another set are joined on this giving the term 'long line'.

On our passage out we met the Looe lugger *Our Girls* who was on her way home and showed us the good catch she had made. Her skipper pointed to the sky as we passed and he knew, as we did, that the weather was going to be bad but with our line baited we had little choice but to shoot it over the side. We completed this just before dark which was a good thing because when flinging the hooks over it's very easy to get hooked oneself. After the shoot the crew washed down decks, stowed the baskets securely and then went below for a meal. After two hours it was time to haul in using a motor line hauler to do the hard job of bringing it up from the sea bed. The fishing was not very good but by now we were more concerned with getting everything aboard, stowed away, and setting out for home. It took us nearly six hours to recover all the gear and by this time the weather was really bad.

We finally started off but shaping course for the Eddystone in the dark with the wind coming at us from a westerly direction, hitting the port bow, it was not easy to spot a really heavy sea coming along. After an hour of battering one very big roller caught us and breaking over the bulwarks it filled the deck forward, lifting off the fish room hatch. This allowed a lot of water to go below where it swirled through the ship and reached the engine room under the wheelhouse aft. Both flywheels were under water and the motors soon stopped as the ignition systems became wet. As luck would have it at this time we had a third engine fitted in a separate compartment forward and this kept ticking over merrily. This gave us enough power to heave to putting the boat gently into the wind and we set to pumping out. The after engines being warm soon dried out and *Our Daddy* was once again under way for home but keeping off course a point or two to ease her along over the worst seas. Two hours later the Eddystone light flashed up in the distance and very thankfully we were nearing home. There is no doubt that had we taken that sea in an undecked boat instead of a decked lugger a disaster would have occured.

Shortly after the last war we were operating from Plymouth and in company with boats from most of the Westcountry fleets we were spread out over a wide area looking for signs for drift net fishing. Towards the late afternoon vessels began to concentrate about four miles S.E. of the Eddystone and when we closed with them we could see all the indications of palagic fish present. Gannets were diving, a small whale was blowing and the water looked oily and smelt strongly of fish. Towards evening in the gathering dusk the various boats began taking up positions to shoot their nets but it was not easy with so many in close company to keep clear of one another. We shot our nets on the landward side of the fleet and as the daylight faded hundreds of seagulls were heard screeching over the boats to the south of us. Shoals of fish were swimming strongly in that direction and with their combined force they were bringing the bottom of the nets to the surface where they became wrapped around the headrope several times over with the fish enmeshed, looking like a long silver balloon on the water.

Our first shoot was a failure but many boats had got good catches and were soon on the way home, it was just the luck of the draw. Our second shoot was not much better and then on our little radio we heard that gale force winds were rapidly approaching from a southerly direction. The impending gale had been sensed by the fish and as we searched around we came across areas of sea that looked like the boil of a rip tide where masses of fish were swimming around in circles. We had found the fish but dare we risk a shoot as often in these conditions the nets would be thrown together and in any case the threat of bad weather hung over us also. I decided to shoot part of our nets and take a chance so we turned with the wind behind us and streamed a drogue or sea anchor to keep us from blowing ahead too fast in the stiffening breeze. Having shot a third of our net a long rope was secured to the headrope and the ship brought round into wind. She was made fast to the net by the bow and a mizzen set aft to keep her head on. We had to have one engine in forward gear all the time to ease the strain of the boat pulling back from the net in the bad weather. By now all the other boats had gone back to harbour and even the large Plymouth trawlers had returned to port. As the wind freshened it started raining which did not improve our lot so we had a quick mug of tea and a snack to cheer us up a bit.

We had not removed our oilskins and were soon ready to haul in and that was when the trouble started. The nets had all bunched up with the floats, normally spaced on the surface six fathoms apart, now all in a heap. It was not really surprising after shooting through that mass of fish and the easiest thing to have done would have been to cut loose and run for port. Fortunately we had a motorised capstan on the foredeck so we prepared to hoist the nets on board with the main halyard tackle and using the winch. We were able lump by lump and full of mackerel to hoist the net over the bulwark and then down on to the foredeck.

All this took several hours and by that time we had a southerly gale. We lowered the mizzen sail, chose the right moment, then turned the boat to run before the wind and sea for home. After an hour I realised that to make for Looe would be dangerous in the dark with a heavy sea and the wind in that quarter. By the time we reached there it would be an ebb tide coming out of the river and to cross in over the bar with breaking seas might be disastrous. So we squared away for Plymouth where the breakwater light was beckoning on the starboard bow in the distance. The after cabin hatch was closed down in case a sea broke in over the stern but by the time we got in past Rame Head, the ebb tide was coming out and a breaking sea was reaching across from Penlee buoy. End on to sea however, the *Our Daddy* is a good sea boat and she brought us in to Plymouth quite safely although the greatest danger at such times is engine or steering gear breakdown. We could do nothing about the nets on deck, full of fish, until daylight, when all in good time we cleared out and sold the catch.

Although we have been caught out in bad weather we have learnt to study some of the signs that nature has provided as advance warnings. A rapid rise or fall in the movements of the barometer are not good omens and after a period of bad weather it is better to see a gradual rise over a few days. During the winter one or two frosty nights in succession warns of an approaching back or south westerly wind and hail showers also foretell it will blow from this quarter. A cloud formation like a long bar to the south or westward is a warning of rain and south westerlies within twenty four hours. This cloud type is known locally as 'Jack Eddy's Bars' and is sometimes seen on fine days. With an offshore wind a cloud will be seen to be gradually dispersing as it drifts out to sea until there is nothing left and this is yet again a sign of approaching wind from the south or south west. Jack Eddy's Bars seen in the east portend an easterly wind and a large anvil shaped cloud means squally weather with strong winds. A 'sunspot' seen close on either side of the sun is usually a bad sign and it looks like a small section of rainbow. Sometimes approaching bad weather is indicated by a large halo or circle around the sun. At night one may see a small star close to the moon which again means bad weather. The air temperature will often give a warning of impending weather changes. Many people who suffer from rheumatism will sense when there is going to be a change by their own feelings.

The reader may well ask, "Are there no signs of a spell of good weather?" Yes, of course there are. The finest conditions that one can expect come during the summer months in what is known to us as a round wind. All day a light wind comes from the direction of the sun, starting from the east in the morning and then following the arc of the sun across the sky so that it is southerly at midday and westerly in the evening. As the sun goes down the wind will drift off the land often bringing with it the scent of hay, freshly cut and this is a sure sign of a good spell. These signs and portends are what we have learnt locally but if you make observations in your own area you may find many apply elsewhere.

Superstition is very strong in the minds of many fishermen and I am afraid that I am no exception. It is considered bad to launch a new boat on a Friday, or to commence a fishing season on a Friday. Some object to taking a Parson to sea and certain items of food are taboo, but the most common superstition among our men is the bunny rabbit. We hate to hear it mentioned at sea, or on shore, and one can receive a very black look and expect to be admonished severely should you talk about it in front of fishermen. These superstitions have been handed down through the ages in the fishing fleets. Here follows two strange but true coincidences.

The Eddystone Rocks seen at the end of the last century, note the old steamer. The large bells have since been removed after the installation of a modern foghorn. The old base on the left is the remains of Smeaton's Tower, a previous lighthouse which was removed and rebuilt on Plymouth Hoe.

My eldest grandson, Paul, had two tame rabbits and knowing of these superstitions for quite some time had been asking me to come up to his home to see them. After many repeated invitations, I said, "Now look Paul, if I come up to see them, they won't live long". At which he laughed. However, one evening, my wife and I went up to my son Terry and his wife Jean's house. Whilst sitting down and in conversation, the door opened and in came Paul with his two rabbit in his arms to show me. Everyone had a jolly good laugh about it, but within two days both were dead, for no apparent reason, even though I had wished them no harm at the time!!

The Lyons Club of Looe had permission to use a large field owned by one of its members, Mr. Jim Philip, farmer, near Pelynt, for a fund raising effort. In the evening my wife and I went along to see the fun. There were many different kinds of competitions going on with a very large crowd of people. On going down through the centre of the field we saw managing one small enclosure the familiar figures of Dr. Gates and his wife. As we came near, he called, "Come on A.J. Have a go". The small circle enclosure with a three foot fence around housed three or four rabbits. There were several china plates around the inside with lettuce leaves on each. One had to pay and guess which plate of lettuce would be attacked when the game started and the bunnies were placed down inside the enclosure. As a friend of our family for many years, he already knew the story of my Grandson's rabbits. I said to him, "You know what will happen!" With a grin on his face he accepted my entrance fee, needless to say, I did not win the game, so we carried on to other competitions forgetting the bunny game.

Two days later, in the morning, I was on the quay at East Looe, Dr. Gates was calling to me, whilst sitting in his car. When I got close he said, looking rather subdued, "It happened that the bunny died the day after, I had only borrowed it for the day, it was a family pet!" I did not know what to say, except that I was sorry the bunny had died.

It is true like many other fishermen, that I am very superstitious about these things and although a life-time fisherman, I could neither harm an animal or a bird of any kind. There is the saying that truth is stranger than fiction, I think perhaps through the years I have seen this also.

One of the great signposts of the sea is the Eddystone lighthouse. We set course by it but are apt to take it for granted when we should perhaps sometimes think and consider what a wonderful piece of work it is. The present tower was built in less than three years (1878-1882) by James Douglass and stands on rocks twelve miles off Looe. It is reputed to be the farthest from shore of any lighthouse in the United Kingdom. The solid cylindrical base is forty two feet in diameter and the lantern is 136 ft. above sea level, at high water. It is constructed of 2,171 granite blocks quarried in Cornwall and Scotland each weighing two to three tons and carefully shaped to interlock and then cemented. The total weight is 4,668 tons and nothing would ever move the structure. There are large water tanks in the base holding a years supply. Entry is by a metal door at the base which itself weighs one ton and stone stairs climb inside the walls to the rooms near the top. Above the living quarters is a small room with a fixed lamp which shines out across an area known as the hand deeps and at night this is very useful as a guide to us fishermen for long lining on these rocks for conger, ling and pollack. In the lantern room above the main lamp shows a beam which is visible for 17½ miles and this has a cycle of a 2½ seconds flash — 4 seconds blank — 2½ seconds flash — 21 seconds blank, etc. During the last few years the Eddystone has played a very important role in our lives which was never foreseen when it was built. On many occasions our inshore fishing has been despoiled by foreign vessels but in 1964 a limit of 12 miles was imposed on these operations. The next step was a declaration that as the Eddystone was built on rocks which were never submerged even at high tides it constituted a point of land and this ruled out any foreign ships from fishing between the lighthouse and the coast and in fact for six miles outside the reef on which it stands. It has therefore proved a saviour to us in more ways than one and long may its light continue to shine and guide those who go down to the sea in ships.

But now once again dramatic changes have taken place in the pattern of fishing off the Cornish coast. During the last three seasons there has been mass exploitation of the mackerel stocks by large deep sea trawlers many of which have been driven down from the North Sea after the loss of fishing rights and the imposition of limits in those waters, also with purse seiners which seem to engage in what may be termed day and night ad lib fishing scooping up the fish like some massive vacuum cleaner with no regard for its effect on the stocks. The bulk of the 'catch' is then transferred to eastern block factory ships which spend the winter months anchored in Cornish bays and the processed fish are then sent in the main to African states. Often when operating in this way many mackerel are scooped up which are not satisfactory and these are dumped overboard and it is known that certain areas of the sea bed have been littered with small and immature dead fish. The season 1978-79 has so far been the worst for this practice and our inshore mackerel boats are being driven out of business.

Fortunately in true inshore fishermen's tradition they have been able to turn over to other fishing and in the last two years the Looe fleet have been scallop dredging during the summer and bottom trawling in the winter and this has produced a good living so far even encouraging some to purchase larger boats designed for this work. Nevertheless many more regulations must be imposed on both foreign and British boats to restrict the amounts grabbed from the sea or the stocks will become 'fished out'. It matters little to the Cornish fishermen whether their livelihood has been ruined by a foreign or British vessel. Usually no move is made by Government departments until the scientists have proved that a species has been overfished and by that time it will be too late to save it. In my opinion there must be an enforced 12 mile limit for all vessels of any nationality which are heavy beam trawlers or purse seiners etc. which are destructive methods of fishing either of the fish stocks or of the sea bed. Outside of this limit there should be controlled operations, rationalised to the requirements of the market. When one realises that the large mackerel now being caught have taken 12-15 years to mature it needs little imagination to see the ultimate result if things continue as they are.

So I come to the end of my story. I have endeavoured to relate and give an impression, in my humble way, of my experiences as a Cornish fisherman over half a century. I sincerely hope that the reader has not been bored by the necessity sometimes for a repetition but I have left out much to try and avoid this. Please accept that this has been written by an ordinary fisherman in his own style and not by an accomplished author.

Alfred John Pengelly and his son, Terry, in happy mood in the wheelhouse of Our Daddy.

Building a Looe lugger: (above) A break during an early stage in construction. (below) The newly completed hull of FY201 Progress, *on the quay, ready for launching and fitting out. (Builder: A Collings)*

LOOE LUGGERS 1900 to 1971   compiled by Arthur Collings.

BUILT FOR SAILING

BUILDER – Tom Pearce

BOAT OWNER	NAME	NUMBER
J.E. Pengelly	Primrose	FY 78
R. Pengelly	Glory	FY 112
C. Prynn	Cuckoo	FY 22
J. Little	Irex	FY 84
R. Pengelly	Undine	FY 726
T. Prynn	L.T.B.	FY 204
S. Symons	Mabel	FY 176
T. Prynn	Beatrice Ann	FY 77
T.H. Pengelly	Olive	FY 108
W. Dan	Henrietta	FY 113
A. West	Gannet	FY 111
J. Pape	Silver Star	FY 93
R. Marshall	Pet	FY 56
J. Richards	R.K.	FY 157
R. Pengelly	Chicken	FY 65
N. Toms	Little Charlie	FY 52
A. Marshall	Galatea	FY 74
D. Little	Florrie	FY 746
J. Symons	Myrtle	FY 43
T. Pengelly	Victoria	FY 19
W. Bowden	Willie	FY 12
R. Dan	Eliza Jane	FY 90
J. Toms	Little May	FY 118
J. Toms	Little Ellen Louise	FY 101
R. Clements	Prairie Flower	FY 154
R. Clements	Elizabeth Ann	FY 743
W. Pengelly	Skitten	FY 88
J. Little	Lorna	FY 85
E. Pengelly	J.T.C.	FY 293
R. Prynn	Agenora	FY 137
J.E. Pengelly	Sparkler	FY 87
W. Davey	Striver	FY 41

BUILDER – P. Ferris

R. Dan	Talisman	FY 242
J. Richards	Valkyrie	FY 243
W. Dan	Elfrida	FY 224
J. Fletcher	Trinket	FY 255
T.J. Stephens	Searchlight	FY 124
J. Webber	Water Lily	FY 121
W. Pengelly	Guide Me	FY 233
T. Fletcher	Leader	FY 287
R. Clements	Billy Bray	FY 333
Jim Soady	Mona	FY 32
F. Pengelly	Harvest Home	FY 159
R. Marshall	Edith Constance	FY 64

BUILDER – R. Pearce

A. Southern	Twilight	FY 334
T. Bartlett	Phantom	FY 250
T.H. Bettinson	Little Gem	FY 24
J. Dove	Minnie	FY 222
W. Davey	Smiling Morn	FY 46
G.W. Pengelly	Our Boys	FY 221
R. Prynn	Kathleen	FY 210
H. Solt	Mayflower	FY 70
J. Jago	Lead Me	FY 382

BUILDER – J. Angear

R. Stephens	Greta	FY 380
J. Hoskin	Welcome	FY 182
J.E. Hoskin	John Wesley	FY 35
G.W. Pengelly	Vera	FY 240
J. Wynhall	Shamrock	FY 45
R. Pengelly	May Blossom	FY 51
R. Pengelly	Janie	FY 371
T. Soady	Guiding Star	FY 363
E. Pengelly	Kindly Light	FY 83
E. Pengelly	Onward	FY 166
J. Pengelly	Evelyn	FY 341
R. Prynn	Ida	FY 340
Ned Tambling	Gleaner	FY 72
J.E. Pengelly	Sweet Home	FY 221
H. Prynn	Anemone	FY 29
A. Collings	Arthur	FY 254

BUILT FOR SAIL AND MOTOR

BUILDER – A. Collings

E.W. Pengelly	Girl Vine	FY 88
R. Pengelly	Janie	FY 227
R. Prynn	Kathleen	FY 297
E. Soady/Ned Ham	Adela	FY 169
H. Butters	Progress	FY 201

BUILDER – R. Pearce

J. Toms	Forget-me-not	FY 377
J. Toms	Forget-me-not	FY 269
J. Toms	Ellen Louise	FY 403
Jim Soady	Gracie	FY 315
J.E. Pengelly	Our Daddy	FY 7
Atkinson	Seagull	FY 408
J.R. Atkinson	Swift	FY 405
T.H. Pengelly	I.R.I.S.	FY 357

French trawler Marguarite *in Talland Bay on March 3rd 1922. She ran ashore in fog later becoming a total loss but the crew were taken off by the Looe lifeboat.*

The schooner Maid *ashore at Hannafore in 1930. She misjudged a very strong wind when trying to make Looe harbour.*

LOOE FISHERMEN'S NICK NAMES

Many of the fishermen in the town have the same surname and in many cases the same christian name that in order to differentiate it has become the custom, over several generations, to give them nick names. Here is a list but it is not claimed to be complete.

Fred Bartlett	*Fip*	George Bartlett	*Clickey*	Herbert Bartlett	*Sherbert*
Jack Bartlett	*Cherry*	Ernest Bettison	*Sussa*	Harry Bettison	*Shellback*
Charlie Bowden	*Chewie*	Jack Bowden	*Squinty*	Harold Butters	*Nibbins*
Jim Butters	*Captain*	Arthur Clements	*Kimina*	Jack Clements	*Coal Jack*
Tom Cox	*Tiddly*	William Cox	*Fadder*	Edwin Dan	*Snaker*
Harry Dan	*Ibbidy*	Bill Davey	*Billy Winker*	Joe Davey	*Dinah*
Albert Dingle	*Abedie*	Reg Dingle	*Kosher*	Alfred Hoskin	*Chid*
Charlie Hoskin	*Cholla*	Charlie Hoskin	*Snip*	John Edward Hoskin	*Gimlet*
Jack Jagoe	*Cuckoo*	Richard Marshall	*Dickey Mouse*	George Martin	*Piggy*
William Pearn	*Wibbs*	James Pearce	*Jimmy Kitty*	Percy Pearce	*Rip*
Charlie Prynn	*Shrimpy*	Leo Prynn	*Tod*	Tommy Prynn	*Cobby*
Arthur Sammells	*Fisher*	Albert Sargent	*Derby*	Bill Sargent	*Willo*
Alfie Soady	*Dalla*	Arthur Soady	*Tommer*	George Soady	*Shoot Bob*
George Soady	*Winker*	Jack Soady	*Nuggie*	Jim Soady	*Jimmits*
Fernley Soady	*Lishey*	Alfred Southern	*Leggy*	Harry Southern	*Admiral*
Ralph Southern	*Bommer*	Laurence Southern	*Rubber*	Dick Stephens	*Polly*
Richard Stephens	*Snippy*	Dick Symons	*Daisy*	Bill Tambling	*Barrier*
Cyril Tambling	*Sir Nick*	Edwin Tambling	*Scruffer*	Ernie Tambling	*Gannet*
Philip Tambling	*Moosh*	Stanley Tambling	*Bantham*	Tom Tambling	*Rock*
Albert Toms	*Boomer*	Bill Toms	*Tucker*	Edgar Toms	*Tit*
Edwin Toms	*Eshwin*	Ernest Toms	*Figgies*	Frank Toms	*Monkey*
Harry Toms	*Trixie*	Reg Toms	*Topsy*	Thomas Toms	*Tommy Pint*
Walter Toms	*Watt*	Bill Taylor	*Rufus*	Ned Taylor	*Finnion*
Charlie Williams	*Black Conger*	Jack Whynall	*Cracky*		

THE PENGELLYS

Albert	*Juice*	Albert	*Amy Walters*	Alfred	*Banes*
Alfred	*Spencer*	Bob	*Bob Walters*	Charles	*Swindow*
Ernest	*Dorman*	Edward	*Tufty*	George	*Georgie Pie*
Jack	*Jacketts*	James	*Nubbies*	John	*Tidla Boggie*
John	*Johnny Dite*	Leo	*Ugh*	Luther	*Acker*
Morris	*Moddow*	John Edward	*Ginger*	John Edward	*Oyster*
Richard	*Old Daddy*	Richard	*Dick Clubs*	Thomas Henry	*Tom Hearl*
Thomas	*Muggie*	Wilfred	*Ike*	William Henry	*Buzzer*
William	*Bill Pie*	William	*Billy Fire Out*		

A line up of many of the older fishermen listed above.

The exact date of this incident is unknown but it must have been towards the end of the 1914-18 war as I remember it as a youngster. Early one morning as dawn was breaking our small inshore crabbers had left the harbour for the grounds to haul in their pots. It was a lovely day with light winds. Not far from shore they were surprised to come across a sailing trawler under full canvas and went alongside to hail the crew but received no response. They boarded the vessel but found not a living soul aboard except a live and well-fed cat. It was reminiscent of the Marie Celeste *of old. She was brought into Looe and is seen above touching the river bed with her keel and as the tide rose she was gently taken up stream and moored alongside the quay. The craft was found to be the* Smiling Morn *of Brixham and her crew had abandoned her out in the Channel thinking she was sinking after a collision with another ship. No doubt there were some red faces and burning ears in Brixham when she was later sailed there by a crew who came down to Looe to fetch her complete with cat.*